Contents

MICHAEL FREEMAN

Atlas of NAZI GERMANY

A Political, Economic and Social Anatomy of the Third Reich

Second edition

Consulting Editor to the first Edition – Tim Mason

LONGMAN
London and New York

Longman Group Limited,
Longman House, Burnt Mill,
Harlow, Essex CM20 2JE, England
and Associated Companies throughout the world.

Published in the United States of America
by Longman Publishing, New York

First published by Croom Helm, 1987
Second edition published by Longman Group Limited, 1995

ISBN 0 582 23924 9 PPR

British Library Cataloguing-in-Publication Data

A catalogue record for this book is
available from the British Library

Library of Congress Cataloging-in-Publication Data

Freeman, Michael J., 1950–
    Atlas of Nazi Germany: a political, economic, and social anatomy
of the Third Reich/Michael Freeman.
        p.   cm.
    Includes bibliographical references and index.
    ISBN 0-582-23924-9
    1. Germany–Historical geography.   2. Germany–Historical geography–
Maps.   3. Germany–History–1933–1945.   I. Title.
    DD256.5.F73354   1995
    943.086′022′3–dc20   94-47233
                                                                                                CIP
                                                                                                AC

Set by 7R in 10/12pt Times
Produced through Longman Malaysia, CL

Foreword to first edition

Mainstream historians do not usually attach much importance to visual images. Their source materials are for the most part written documents, and they produce books which are above all to be read. To try to understand social and political history is to engage in an activity which is above all literary. It is the words which count. The illustrations contained in works of history are perhaps a little more numerous now than they were fifteen years ago, but they are still normally very few and very conventional and are in every sense separate from the text. Modern historians may use old photographs to give an impression of what people, streets, workplaces or warfare looked like, but they seldom use them as evidence or discuss their messages.

Meanwhile, new historical specialisms are arising, which, modelled, it seems, on the history of, and do indeed give appropriate importance to the history of design, of photography, the cinema and television etc., but tend to carry their subject matter away from the concerns of the general historian. Such specialists have a lot to say about how to analyse images from the past, but much less about the use of images in enhancing historical understanding. The visual component in the process of learning about the past thus tends to be underestimated and neglected all round.

In this respect, Michael Freeman's book about Nazi Germany is innovative. It is much more than an historical atlas: he has succeeded in representing most of the important themes in the political, economic and military history of the Third Reich in the form of diagrams, charts, graphs and tables, as well as of maps and photographs. These images are an integral part of what he has written on each theme. His historical summaries comment on the material, and the images document part of his exposition or argument. He has composed the book in a highly self-conscious and deliberate manner which has involved much research and a great deal of painstaking revision in order to reach the best possible relationship between text and image on each spread of pages.

The book is intended for sixth-formers, university students and serious general readers. (Those looking for another picture book on Nazi Germany should stop reading here.) And they will be among the best judges of the value of his approach. Professional experts on recent European history will find some summaries of recent research and debates, and they may also extend their knowledge of the geography of Germany; above all, however, they may come to appreciate, as I have done, how complicated historical issues can be illuminated and clarified when they are presented as a combination of image and prose, diagram and description.

Perhaps it is helpful to give an example of this from my own work. In the past fifteen years some historians of Nazi Germany have come to attach great significance to the fluidity of the institutions of the dictatorship. The processes of decision-making and the channels of command were anything but uniform and clear, and the various ministries, party agencies, military and police authorities devoted great energy and ingenuity to competing with each other for a greater share of the expanding dictatorial powers of the regime. These conflicts probably (not every historian agrees) had a considerable influence over the policies finally sanctioned or chosen by Hitler. The relevant facts and the interpretations to which they give rise are complicated and often technical; many detailed monographs have been written around the theme, but it remains difficult to give a summary account of this aspect of the Third Reich which is intelligible to non-experts. Such accounts, my own included, are all too often congested and allusive, strenuous efforts to make language adequate to the tortuous growth processes of the regime and its policies *in general*. How much clearer all this becomes when we are presented with a series of maps and diagrams which turn 'overlapping jurisdictions' and 'confused patterns of power and responsibility' into visual realities. The abstract nouns gain enormously from being illustrated.

This is the main reason why I believe that Michael Freeman's book will be useful and instructive. He makes difficult and important topics accessible to readers who may not yet know a great deal about Nazi Germany, without in any way condescending to them in the manner typical of popularisers.

Tim Mason
Rome, September 1986

Preface to first edition

This book started life over an impromptu lunchtime discussion with David Croom in the spring of 1984. It was originally intended as a short, popular exposition on the Third Reich, but under Tim Mason's editorial eye and as a result of a certain internal momentum, it turned out to be rather more serious in intent and coverage. However, restrictions of time and money rendered it impossible to make a comprehensive search for *original cartographic* materials. None of the relevant United States archives was searched, for example. In Germany, the only repository examined was the *Bundesarchiv*, which proved to have a disappointingly restricted set of material relating specifically to the National Socialist regime, although it is clear that some items lie in special archival groups like the Speer Collection. The greater body of original cartographic sources has been found, in fact, in Oxford, in the map collections of the Bodleian Library and the School of Geography. Some of these materials were collected in the normal run of accessions, notably up to 1939. Other material was acquired relatively recently from the Directorate of Military Survey. Some also derives from the period during the war when the School of Geography was a centre of naval intelligence work, particularly for the compilation of some of the *Admiralty Handbooks*, although those covering Germany were completed in Cambridge where, unhappily, few records survive. For the rest of the book's illustrative material, it will become immediately apparent that, apart from official printed sources such as the *Statistisches Jahrbuch*, there is a heavy reliance on existing published work. The range of this is enormous and was the primary cause of the extension from one to two years in the time taken to complete the book. It is the individuals whose names are credited on the illustrations who warrant the first acknowledgement. Without their research and writing effort, the book would have been a far more difficult task. If the results of their research have been misdirected or misused in any way, I can but offer apologies and beg the chance to rectify it in later editions. Special thanks must go also to the librarians and library staffs who have assisted me in searches for literature, particularly Rosamund Campbell at St Anthony's College, Oxford, which houses a remarkable special collection on the Third Reich, and Elspeth Buxton at the School of Geography. Gordon Smith, of Keble College, Oxford, suggested various improvements to the text, particularly in those parts dealing with the war. David Croom, of Croom

Helm, has been a marvellous stimulant to the project, in material as well as in mental ways. However, my deepest gratitude must be reserved for Tim Mason, who has been ever patient, always exacting in comment and criticism, and adept at giving encouragement when interest or confidence flagged. I absolve him of all responsibility for any weaknesses in the book. It is first and foremost my own creation. But it would have been measurably inferior without his enormous fund of knowledge, his scholarship and his acuteness of perception.

The illustrations have all been drawn by Jayne Lewin, who has handled the task with characteristic patience and good sense. The transformations from author's 'roughs' into finished products have sometimes been remarkable to see.

I am also grateful to Andrew Goudie, Professor of Geography at Oxford, for the general support that he has enabled me to have in the School of Geography there. The University of Oxford also helped by making travel funds available for my research in Germany.

Michael Freeman
Oxford, September 1986

Preface to second edition

The first edition of this book was out of print in the United Kingdom within three years of its original publication. Preliminary steps were taken in 1990 for Routledge (Croom Helm's successor publisher) to produce a second edition, only to abandon the proposal a year later. It is in this context that I must thank my colleague, John Stevenson, for introducing me to Andrew MacLennan of Longman and helping to set in motion a new edition under a different imprint.

The overall format of the book has remained unchanged and the bulk of the illustrative material has been reproduced in unmodified form, except where the shift from two- to one-colour printing necessitated alterations for reasons of interpretative clarity. The principal revisions have been textual ones, to try to accommodate the continuing additions to the already vast literature of the Nazi regime. A number of sections (for example, that dealing with the war itself – Part Five) survive relatively intact. But others (for example, Part Three on Society) have been very substantially modified in the light of recent research.

The revision has been greatly helped by the formidable library resources available to me in the University of Oxford. I am grateful to Peter Hayward, Senior Cartographer at the School of Geography, who organised the reproduction of the illustrative material in one-colour form and made necessary alterations. Finally, I must thank Tim Kirk, author of *The Longman Companion to Nazi Germany*, for reading over the revised text and offering comments accordingly. The original role of consulting editor was performed by the late Tim Mason. His Foreword to the first edition is reproduced here and I must once again record the enormous measure of his input when the original book was compiled. Moreover, in making the revision, I have returned to the many notes and letters that Tim wrote in response to my various first drafts. They have been a renewed source of comment and inspiration.

Michael Freeman
Oxford, June 1994

Acknowledgements

The publishers would like to thank the Bodleian Library for their permission to reproduce illustrative material: Figures 3.12, 3.13 and 3.14 from pages 45, 242 and 347 in *Die Kunst im Dritten Reich* (1938), Shelfmark *Per.17007.c.35.* and Figure 3.19 from page 30 in *Der Nationalsozialistische Schulungsbrief* (June 1934), Shelfmark *1170.c.5.*

Abbreviations

BVP   *Bayerische Volkspartei* – Bavarian People's Party

DAF   *Deutsche Arbeitsfront* – German Labour Front

DAW   *Deutsche Ausrustungswerke Gmbh* – German Armaments Works: a division of the SS organisation

DDP   *Deutsche Demokratische Partei* – German Democratic Party

DEST   *Deutsche Erd und Steinwerke Gmbh* – German Earth and Stone Works: a division of the SS organisation

DNVP   *Deutschnationale Volkspartei* – German National People's Party

DVP   *Deutsche Volkspartei* – German People's Party

EHER-Verlag – NSDAP's central publishing house in Munich

GBA   *Generalbevollmächtiger für den Arbeitseinsatz* – General Plenipotentiary for Labour Allocation

Gestapo   *Geheimesstaatspolizei* – Secret State Police

HJ   *Hitler Jugend* – Hitler Youth organisation

KdF   *Kraft durch Freude* – Strength through Joy: the leisure organisation of the German Labour Front (DAF)

KPD   *Kommunistische Partei Deutschlands* – German Communist Party

KRIPO   *Kriminalpolizei* – Criminal Police

NSBO   *Nationalsozialistische Betriebszellenorganization* – Nazi factory cell organisation

NSDAP   *Nationalsozialistische Deutsche Arbeiter Partei* – National Socialist German Workers' Party (Nazi Party)

NSKK   *Nationalsozialistische Kraftfahrer Korps* – National Socialist Motor Transport Corps

NSV   *Nationalsozialistische Volkswohlfahrt* – National Socialist Public Welfare Organisation

OKW   *Oberkommando der Wehrmacht* – Armed Forces High Command

RFSS   *Reichsführer-SS* – Himmler's title as SS Chief

RKFDV   *Reichskommisar für die Festigung deutschen Volkstums* – Reich Commissar for the Strengthening of German Nationhood

RSHA   *Reichssicherheitshauptamt* – Main Reich Security Office, the apex of the SS organisation

RUSHA   *Rasse- und Siedlungs-Hauptamt* – SS main office for race and settlement

SA   *Sturmabteilungen* – Stormtroopers: the strong-arm squads of the Nazi Party

SD   *Sicherheitsdienst* – Security Service of the SS

SPD *Sozialdemokratische Partei Deutschlands* – German Social Democratic Party

SS *Schutzstaffeln* – Guard detachments: more widely, the Nazis' elite formations

USCHLA   *Untersuchungs- und Schlichtungs-Ausschuss* – NSDAP investigation and arbitration committee

USPD *Unabhangige Sozialdemokratische Partei Deutschlands* – Independent Social Democratic Party of Germany

WVHA   *Wirtschafts und Verwaltungshaupamt* – the chief SS economic and administrative office

Introduction

Almost a decade has passed since the substance of this book was first compiled.[1] In that time, what was recently unthinkable has become reality: the two Germanies are now one. The phenomenon of German division and the existence of a communist-controlled regime in the east, the German Democratic Republic, was for more than 40 years a potent reminder of the legacy of National Socialism. The dramatic collapse of that regime in 1989/90 and the subsequent movement towards unification lead some to think that the Nazi era would at last be able to pass into history. But such a view has proved naïve to say the least. The emergence of a new German national state not only raised elsewhere in Europe questions about the hegemonic potential (especially in economic terms) of a country of some 78 million people, but also threw the spotlight back on to the historical experience of the unified German state in the sense of Germans recovering a measure of historical continuity or legitimacy. The years of the Nazi dictatorship have thus re-emerged upon the contemporary agenda, dramatically enhanced at times by the protests and mob violence of Neo-Nazi groups, particularly in the east, where the ending of years of political repression has exposed the frustrations of youth, intensified in turn by the destruction of normality and the uncertain prospects of life dominated by a prosperous and powerful neighbour, the former Federal Republic.

Against this backdrop, the literature on Nazi Germany continues to accumulate in burgeoning fashion. The demise of communism has also aided this process in another sense: increasing bodies of archival materials have now become freely accessible in ways that were not so before. The literature, too, remains – as was remarked upon in the book's first edition – characterised by intense and often bitter controversy. Nowhere was this apparent than in the *Historikerstreit*, a battle or quarrel about the Germans' understanding of their history which raged in the German press over 1986 and 1987.[2] This centred upon attempts to historicise or relativise the Nazi past and upon the resulting accusations of trivialisation that such efforts brought, particularly in relation to the Holocaust. Some commentators have since come to regard the *Historikerstreit* as superfluous,[3] in that it merely reflected, if in particularly acutely contested form, what were already recognised as long-standing questions in the writing of history, of Nazi history especially. According to Kershaw, these comprise three basic dimensions: historical–philosophical, political/ideological, and moral.[4] They help to explain why, as the first edition of this book remarked, surveys of the historiography of the Third Reich take the appearance of a never-ending Agatha Christie novel. The succession of events and processes continues to be re-examined, re-sorted and re-located to make for new readings of the plot such that any intelligible dénouement becomes steadily more remote. Kershaw, in his latest exhaustive, if exhausting, account puts it more simply: 'there appears . . . to be an inverse ratio between the massive extension of empirical research on the Third Reich and the embodiment of such research in full-scale synthesis'.[5] For the scions of postmodernism, of course, this signals nothing unsatisfactory. As Harvey records: 'Post-modernism swims, even wallows, in the fragmentary and the chaotic currents of change as if that is all there is.'[6] Lyotard's 'incredulity towards metanarratives' invites dismissal of projects which seek 'synthesis'.[7] The myriad interpretations of and perspectives on the Third Reich offer, in the mould of Derrida, for example, their own distinctive discourse.[8] Not unrelated to the issues of postmodernism is the crisis of representation that has been noted in the social sciences and the humanities.[9] Williams thus attempts to explicate the environmental history of the Black Mountains using the novel form, reconstituting a life-world in which the narrative account is presented from above and below in a manner which does not really admit of closure except in so far as the reader determines.[10] There are senses in which one can see such works as Christabel Bielenberg's *The Past is Myself*[11] or Thomas Keneally's *Schindler's List*[12] as in part echoing the form in the context of knowledge of the Third Reich.

The present book might be viewed as a further experiment in representation in that it seeks to provide a *graphic* account of the outward face and the inward structures of the Third Reich. It tries to portray the Third Reich in ways which provide an immediacy of communication that is achieved only with much more difficulty in the consecutive form of prose. It is a remarkable, and in this writer's view, disconcerting feature of the vast body of the literature on the Third Reich that it is so lacking in graphic representation. Broszat's penetrating and convincing analysis, *The Hitler State*, for example, confines its graphic presentation to Nazi election performance, a single linkage diagram on party-state relations, and tables on the sociological structure of party membership and on political and other crimes.[13] Hidden in both text and footnotes, though, is much statistical and other material which, if it could have been suitably presented, would have lent a greater immediacy and clarity to many of the facets being analysed. The argument may be put that the complexity and constant state of flux of so many structures and organisations of the Third Reich make invalid any semi-formal articulation of them. But the obverse of this argument is that such features lend even greater force to some form of graphic presentation. It may be the case that, metaphorically speaking, the movement of the chess pieces on the board steadily reconstitutes the rules of the game, but this does not render any less valid the identification of the pieces, or of their pattern on the board at any one time and the circumscribing effects that result.

It is not just with 'graphicacy', though, that this book is concerned. More fundamentally, it attempts to expose some of the geographical dimensions of the Third Reich. This does not mean the compilation of some sort of 'place' inventory – although there are elements of this, for example the case of the expanding economic organisation of the *Schutzstafflen* or SS. Nor does it primarily focus on distributional patterns in space, although once again there are examples of this, as in Part Four. It refers most of all to what has come to be described as the dialectics of space. Whereas it has been conventional in western marxism to think only of the dialectics of time, more recently there has been a concern to address the ways in which space forms an active not a passive construct in social production and reproduction. Space is no longer treated as 'the dead, the undialectical, the immobile'.[14] Capitalism sustains itself not just through such mechanisms as time-space annihilation, but through occupying space in the search for renewed means of accumulation.[15] Capitalism, in effect, yields its own *historical geography* as parts of the landscape are successively valued, devalued and revalued in the circulatory ferment.[16] For a state which left the forces of economic production, particularly industrial production, very largely in the hands of private business, the Third Reich forms an apt subject for such a perspective. This can be conceived not just in terms of the familiar thesis that territorial annexation and conquest from 1938 onwards represented an outward resolution of the crises of capital that the Nazi state was undergoing by this time.[17] It can be related also to the internal resolutions or workings of capital, either within the area constituting the Greater German Reich or in the more extended realms of SS domination. There were, for instance, windfall profits to be made in the east through the aryanisation of Jewish businesses and the use of forced labour.[18] This naturally acted to deflect capital away from traditional but less profitable foci of industrial enterprise in areas like the Ruhr.[19] The acquisition of standing iron and steel capacity through annexation and conquest likewise had implications for traditional investment centres, including those which flowed from policies of autarky.

In considering the dialectics of space, however, it is not just upon capital that the focus should rest. It is necessary to look more broadly at the fabric of power, in particular to the four primary power blocks that propelled the Third Reich on its brief historical course: the army, the SS, the state and the Party. Not only is it an essential part of any analysis of the Third Reich to examine the relations and alliances of these blocks and the way the influence of one or other altered as the war progressed, for instance. It is also vital to consider the incongruencies and tensions that flowed from the differing spatial structures through which their powers were exercised. The Third Reich exhibited some remarkably dissonant administrative field systems, as Part Two will endeavour to show.

The most startling geographical feature of the Third Reich was undeniably the scale of its territorial extension and areal conquest. By 1942 it constituted one of the most rapidly made land empires in history. It was over 3,200 kilometres from the German naval bases on the west coast of France to the Russian front in the Don Basin. The furthest longitudinal extent of Versailles Germany was only about 950 kilometres, and even that distance was interrupted by the Polish corridor. The resource value of such a land base for an advanced industrial state like Germany was formidable. But advanced capitalist economies are not made from the simple accumulation of coal, mineral and manufacturing bases, however numerous. They are created, too, through the emergence of complex lineaments of communication, from the working out of myriad systems of comparative advantage, involving production linkages and trading reciprocities of multitudinous form. This provided one of the major difficulties under which the expanded Third Reich laboured. Already in 1939 the communications system of Germany proper (the Altreich) was strained from the expansions and re-orientations that Hitler's re-armament and autarkic policies imposed upon the economy.[20] With the territorial annexations of that period and, later, territorial conquests, the problems intensified. Of course the regime could utilise the communications systems of annexed or occupied territories (though much less easily in Russia, where the wider railway gauge was a severe impediment), but these, and more critically the structures of trade relations, had evolved in the context of largely independent national development. They did not readily interlock into a new style of European industrial economy which was targeted towards German needs and the German core area, following a neo-colonial system of resource assemblage. The Reichsbahn was soon to register these strains as locomotives, rolling stock and manpower was eked out over an increasingly diffuse network and as trans-European line-hauls accumulated in number and scale as the war progressed.[21] The extensive autobahn system that Nazi planners envisaged for central Europe offered a potential solution, but the German autobahn system itself remained very incomplete at the outbreak of war and the completed sections, anyway, were equivocally economic in their objective.[22] Given the Third Reich's transport problems, one would have expected autobahn construction to have been given some priority after 1939; in practice, new construction was almost entirely abandoned.[23]

The exigencies of war, of course, wove their own pattern into these difficulties of resource transfer and assembly. The war fronts required a continuous stream of supplies and materials, food and men. Where attrition formed the primary mould of combat, the front became a bottomless sink into which materials and men were poured. So as trainloads of requisitioned resources and conscripted foreigners rumbled into Germany from former countries of Europe and from Russia, there was a counter-stream of troops and weaponry.

As the Third Reich evolved, therefore, especially after 1936, it was attempting to forge entirely new sets of spatial relations, but it was never fully able to realise or service these, and in this respect it can be argued that distance produced its own tyranny. To borrow the terminology of Le Febvre, Nazi 'representations of space' came into collision with standing 'spatial practices'.[24] Moreover, time proved too short to remould the diverse economic-industrial bases of the annexed and conquered territories into a unitary pan-German system and to evolve a complementary profile of communication and trade infrastructures. The way the traditional dominance of the Ruhr was maintained to the very end of the war demonstrates the regime's relative bankruptcy in remodelling the European economic-industrial realm to meet its purposes more clearly, notwithstanding the legendary efforts of Speer's war ministry to systematise the utilisation of annexed and conquered resource groupings. The Ruhr's position was a very evident strategic weakness, as 1944 and 1945 were to prove.[25] But it also became progressively sub-optimal in location terms as the frontiers of the Reich expanded. The development of a more easterly industrial complex, on the scale of the Ruhr, would have made real sense in terms of the economics and logistics of location. But this ascribes to the Third Reich a dominance of economic purpose which was manifestly absent. Economic optima and economic consistency were frequently and increasingly compromised by ideological designs. In this way, thousands of skilled Jews were deported from vital German and Polish war factories mid-way through the war for extermination in death camps like Auschwitz.[26] But even in its progressive drive to liquidate Europe's Jews, the regime was caught in the same distance web as that experienced in the economic-industrial system. SS demands for deportation trains to serve points as far afield as south-west France and southern Greece merely exacerbated the Reichsbahn's many problems. And it was not just through racial ideology that economic efficiency was compromised. As Peukert has recorded, there was no over-arching role for the state in economic management. The Nazi era effectively saw the 'privatisation' of the state – as state bodies were given quasi-private economic functions and private firms were accorded quasi-state powers.[27] Goering's Four-Year-Plan Organisation exemplified the former, the chemical giant, I-G Farben the latter. The outcome, according to Peukert, was 'a welter of jurisdictions and responsibilities'.[28]

As the Third Reich grew in areal extent, posing all kinds of problems of spatial re-integration on a Europe-wide scale, it was upholding concepts of territory and maintaining maladjusted systems of territorial administration which could only frustrate the difficulties.[29] The singular power of Party Gauleiters, in the style of territorial chieftains, was quite alien to the operation of an advanced industrial state. Speer and his armaments ministry soon found this out to their cost when efforts were begun to harness industrial production more clearly towards the needs of war.[30] In the Gauleiters' view, their territories were not intended to be subservient to any central or Reich authority. The interests of the local party and the well-being of the local population were their primary and sovereign concerns, not the wider workings of the German state, either in peace or in war. Similar centrifugal or divergent tendencies were characteristic of occupied territories where Party strongmen sometimes wielded even greater powers than their counterparts in the Reich proper. The Reichskommissariat of the Ukraine under Erich Koch (contemporaneously Gauleiter of East Prussia) was a particular case in point. And the occupied territories presented an entirely separate problem in the way each displayed variant patterns of government.[31] In this sense, Hitler's great land empire was more a loose federation under the over-arching eye of his leadership than a clearly regulated, purposive colonial realm.

The administration of Germany proper and, later, of the Greater German Reich presented another series of limitations. It was not only the 'Gau-kingdoms' which distracted from orderly *national* government, but the way so few departments of Reich administration operated congruent administrative field systems, a feature that the rapid breakdown of cabinet government tended to cement. Even more critically, none of these systems bore any relationship to the Party Gaue, which were modelled on the Reichstag electoral districts of the 1920s and left largely unchanged until the end of the war. To add to this complexity, moreover, the military operated its own distinctive regional system which was later replicated in the SS. Then there were still the remnants of the Länder which, although emasculated of separate political power in the *Gleichschaltung* of spring 1933, remained as bases for the administration of education and other social services. The outcome was thus a veritable maze of overlapping and often conflicting jurisdictions, as Part Two demonstrates. The Nazi practice, too, of appointing regional Party leaders to approximately parallel state offices added to the confusion rather than reducing it. Some Gauleiters, for example, quickly seized this as a pretext for pursuing their own designs by claiming direct Führer-authority over and above the traditional administrative apparatus of the state.

The quasi-feudalism of the Nazi Gauleiters, along with, for example, the absurd images of medieval chivalry cultivated in higher echelons of the SS,[32] reflected, in a deeper sense, what some have come to regard as one of the most fundamental tensions of modern capitalism: the persistent breaking up of place, of environment-bound traditions, as the forces of capital constantly re-make geographical space.[33] It is in this respect that one can begin to understand the apparent contradiction of a machine state, combining all the latest in science and technology, becoming allied to a racial myth grounded on German soil and in historical legend. The 'Blood and Soil' syndrome, so beloved of Nazi propagandists, can be construed as an attempt to anchor German society in a world that appeared to many to be in a constant state of flux. The achievements of German capitalism in the later nineteenth century were not echoed in the first third of the twentieth. Compounded by defeat in war, German capitalism underwent a succession of crises. It was not just that the lower middle classes saw their savings evaporate in the great inflation but that the entire structure of work and business seemed to be increasingly insecure to many eyes. Thus was born a reactionary modernism which sought to unite not divide class groupings and to do so by invoking the will of the state via the production of an all-embracing social myth.[34] According to Harvey, Heidegger based his allegiance to the principles if not the practices of Nazism on the rejection of universal machine rationality as the basis for modern living, proposing instead a 'counter-myth of rootedness in place and environmentally-bound traditions'.[35] For Heidegger, this was the means to security in a turbulent world. In such a context, the especially reactionary form that constituted National Socialism represented one pathway (albeit devastatingly tragic) towards realisation of Heidegger's project. It was a pathway which carried with it much of the baggage of geopolitical theory, but it has to be understood within the wider framework of the capitalist imperative. As Geiss reminded the antagonists of the *Historikerstreit*, concepts of centre and periphery form an indispensable category of study in the Nazi period.[36] So even for some historians, the dialectics of space cannot be escaped.

If the Third Reich was so riddled with discordant and disintegrative tendencies, whether deriving from the processes of capital, the particular exigencies of war, or the insane demands of racial ideology, it is hard to avoid leaning towards the functionalist or structuralist view of the Third Reich as advocated by Broszat,[37] among others. In fact, it is largely this perspective that informs the present book. Some would argue, of course, that there is, in any case, no credible basis to an intellectual perspective which seeks to *synthesise* diverse views of the nature of the Third Reich. Different or competing interpretations cannot be understood outside of their relational frames or contexts. In geographical terms, few observers can fail to be struck by the way the Nazi empire was endeavouring to make far-reaching alterations to the relationship of the German productive machine to the geographical environment. Policies of economic autarky, areal annexation and conquest, the logistical demands of war on two fronts and an increasingly fractured political dominion, all conspired to make the friction of distance, the dialectics of space, into a stark restricting frame. This was no *tabula rasa*, in other words. And grandiose plans for continental autobahns and super broad-gauge railways offered little compromise.

Notes

1　Freeman, M. (1987). *Atlas of Nazi Germany*. London; New York.
2　See Knowlton, J. and Cates, T. (1993) (trs). *Forever in the Shadow of Hitler*. Atlantic Highlands, NJ.
3　See Fest, J. (1993). Postscript, 21 April 1987, in Knowlton and Cates, op. cit. *Forever in the Shadow of Hitler*, p. 264.
4　Kershaw, I. (1993). *The Nazi Dictatorship: Problems and Perspectives of Interpretation*, 3rd edn. London.
5　Ibid., p. 209.
6　Harvey, D. (1989). *The Condition of Postmodernity: an enquiry into the origins of cultural change*. Oxford, p. 44.
7　Quoted in ibid., p. 45.
8　Ibid., p. 51.
9　See, for example, Berg, D. (1993). Between modernism and postmodernism. *Progress in Human Geography* **18**: 494–5.
10　Williams, R. (1988/1990). *People of the Black Mountains* (2 vols). London.
11　Bielenberg, C. (1968). *The Past is Myself*. London.
12　Keneally, T. (1993). *Schindler's List*. London. (Originally published in 1982 as *Schindler's Ark*.)
13　Broszat, M. (1981). *The Hitler State: the foundation and development of the internal structure of the Third Reich*. London. (Originally published in German in 1969 as *Der Staat Hitlers*.)
14　See Soja, E. (1989). *Post-modern Geographies: the reassertion of space in critical social theory*. London, pp. 10–11, quoting Foucault.
15　See, for example, Smith, N. (1984). *Uneven Development: nature, capital and the production of space*. Oxford, p. 117 ff.
16　See Harvey, D. (1982). *The Limits to Capital*. Oxford, p. 373 ff.
17　See the account in Kershaw, *The Nazi Dictatorship* pp. 52–3, 75–7.
18　The industrialist Oskar Schindler, as recounted in Thomas Keneally's book (see note 12), in many ways encapsulates the trend.
19　See Gillingham, J. R. (1985). *Industry and Politics in the Third Reich: Ruhr coal, Hitler and Europe*. London.

20   See Matthews, H. P. S. and O'Mahony, P. (1939). Germany in April 1939. Unpublished report in the Library of Oxford University Institute of Economics and Statistics Part II: 25–7; see also Robbins, M. (1979). The Third Reich and its Railways. *Journal of Transport History* **5** (new series): 83–90.

21   On 15 December 1942, 54 out of 260 trains crossing German frontiers outwards were locomotive coal trains. See Robbins, *The Third Reich*.

22   See Overy, R. J. (1973). Transportation and re-armament in the Third Reich. *Historical Journal* **16**: 389–409.

23   Ibid.

24   Le Febvre, H. (1991). *The Production of Space*. Oxford, p. 36 ff.

25   See Milward, A. S. (1965). *The German Economy at War*. London, ch. 7; in 1944, of the 166 million tons of German coal production, nearly 111 million were mined in the Ruhr – see Gillingham, *Industry and Politics*, p. 58.

26   See Mason, T. (1972). The primacy of politics – politics and economics in National Socialist Germany. In Turner, H. A. (ed.). *Nazism and the Third Reich*. Oxford, p. 195.

27   Peukert, D. J. K. (1989). *Inside Nazi Germany: conformity, opposition and racism in everyday life*. London, p. 44.

28   Ibid.

29   See Broszat, *The Hitler State*; also Caplan, J. (1977). The Politics of Administration: the Reich Interior Ministry and the German civil service. *Historical Journal* **20**: 707–36.

30   See Milward, *The German Economy at War*, pp. 153–5.

31   See Kirk, T. (1994). *Longman Historical Companion to Nazi Germany*. London, pp. 146–50.

32   Burleigh, M. and Wippermann, W. (1991). *The Racial State: Germany, 1933–45*. Cambridge, pp. 272–4.

33   See Harvey, *The Condition of Postmodernity*, chs 2 and 5.

34   One of the best accounts of the perspective discussed here is Peukert, *Inside Nazi Germany*.

35   Harvey, *The Condition of Postmodernity*, p. 35.

36   Geiss, I. (1993). On the Historikerstreit. In Knowlton and Cates, *Forever in the Shadow of Hitler*, pp. 256–7.

37   Broszat, *The Hitler State*.

Prelude

Prelude

1 *The Weimar Republic*

The Weimar Republic came into being in the midst of the German war defeat in the autumn of 1918. Rising popular disaffection with the military and the monarchy precipitated a revolutionary movement beginning with naval mutinies at Kiel in late October and followed by the rapid establishment of soldiers' and workers' councils throughout most German cities in much the same mould as had occurred in Russia that year. By the second week of November, a reformist socialist government was in place, a republic had been declared, the Kaiser had abdicated and was in exile in Holland, and the army's war leaders had been forced from the centre stage.

The new government proved hardly revolutionary in mould. It was dominated by moderate socialists (SPD) who still clung to elements of the pre-war political scene; indeed, the administrative continuity with the past proved to be one of the most remarkable features of the German revolution. One result was that more revolutionary but minor socialist groups were quickly alienated and, later, were subject to violent suppression, with the help of newly formed army units. The threads of political continuity were reinforced, moreover, when in the first parliamentary election in January 1919, the socialists (SPD and USPD) were able to form a government only with the support of the Catholic Centre Party (Zentrum) and the German Democratic Party (DDP).

The 'Weimar constitution' was adopted by the Reichstag, or Parliament, in August 1919. It was exceptionally democratic in that it gave the vote to all men and women at the age of 20, embraced proportional representation in elections and, more widely, sought to specify the basic rights of citizens in a democratic state. The latter encompassed, for example, the protection of religious freedoms, the facility with which workers could combine, as well as laying out the critical elements of a modern welfare state. Governments were responsible to Parliament and there was to be a strong popularly elected President. Provisions were also made for popular referenda. The relationship between the central government and the sovereign states of Bismarck's Reich was redefined to give much greater control at the centre. The states henceforward became *Länder*, their powers of self-administration

Fig. 0.1 The Länder, and Prussia and its Provinces under Weimar

Länder		
I	Bavaria	
II	Saxony	
III	Württemberg	
IV	Baden	
V	Thuringia	
VI	Hesse	
VII	Hamburg	
VIII	Mecklenburg-Schwerin	
IX	Oldenburg	
X	Brunswick	
XI	Anhalt	

XII	Bremen	
XIII	Lippe	
XIV	Lübeck	
XV	Waldeck	
XVI	Schaumburg-Lippe	
XVII	(Prussia)	

Prussian Provinces	
1	East Prussia
2	Brandenburg
3	Pomerania
4	Grenzmark Posen Westpreussen
5	Silesia
6	Saxony
7	Schleswig-Holstein
8	Hanover
9	Westphalia
10	Hessen-Nassau
11	Rhine Province
12	Hohenzollern

confined to the police, the judiciary and education. In the second parliamentary chamber set up under the Weimar constitution, the *Reichsrat*, the *Länder* supposedly gained a broader measure of influence on government. But, in practice, the Reichsrat was subservient to the Reichstag, which was in turn somewhat overshadowed by the Reich government. For many later commentators, the fatal flaw in the Weimar constitution was the way that it laid out administrative machinery which could be given definition and substance only through subsequent legislative and political decision. In defence, one may say that the constitution was so formed because of the way it sought to reflect competing political pressures. In modern parlance, it allowed for multiple solutions.

The internal political geography of Germany under the Weimar regime was among the most complicated of all contemporary European countries. (Fig. 0.1) Before the birth of Hitler's state, Germany was divided into no less than 17 *Länder*, the largest of which was Prussia, covering some 60 per cent of the country's land area and embracing some 60 per cent of its population. Prussia was itself divided into separate provinces. The remaining *Länder* varied wildly in size and population. Bavaria, for instance, had an area of 78,000 square kilometres and a population of some 8 million, while Schaumburg-Lippe had corresponding figures of 340 and 50,000. The resulting geographical mosaic was predictably very confused. While Prussia was the dominant force across the northern half of the country and Bavaria, by virtue of its large size, likewise in the south, the small German *Länder* were distributed across the face of western Germany, many of them also having detached territorial outliers to add further to the confusion.

Assessments of the Weimar Republic must necessarily consider the various historical exigencies within which it was framed. Few could deny that it was a remarkable experiment in democracy; but it fell victim to both internal antagonisms and those on the wider historical stage, the Versailles peace treaty among them.

2   *Versailles and the Weimar Republic*

The Treaty of Versailles of 1919 redrew the political map of Europe on an unprecedented scale. (Fig. 0.2) For Germany, however, the territorial adjustments required by the Treaty were limited. Alsace-Lorraine was restored to France (having been taken from France in 1871). Minor frontier adjustments were made at Germany's expense in favour of Belgium, Czechoslovakia and Denmark. Territory was lost in the east to the recreated state of Poland, much of it land which had been seized by Prussia in the eighteenth century. But, in total, Germany had to relinquish only 13 per cent of its territory, containing approximately 10 per cent of its population. Alongside the consequences of the Treaties of St Germain and Trianon for the Austro-Hungarian Empire, or compared with the humiliating territorial losses imposed by Germany on Russia at the earlier Treaty of Brest-Litovsk, the German state survived relatively intact, geographically, economically and politically. It deposed its dynasty, replaced monarchy by republic, and in most facets retained its potential as a strong, independent nation.

The German people saw the provisions of Versailles very differently. Upon receipt of the draft terms in May 1919, the first parliamentary government of the Republic resigned, refusing to accede to the terms. German officialdom was well aware of the likely demands of any peace treaty, but the German population at large had accumulated entirely different expectations and had not been discouraged from doing so by the

Fig. 0.2 The Versailles Settlement

government. The terms of the Treaty thus came as a profound shock. Many Germans were incensed by the detachment of East Prussia in order to create the Polish sea corridor. Equivalent bitterness arose from the requirement that Germany accept responsibility for starting the war (the war guilt clause) and deliver vast reparations; many Germans believed that they had fought for defensive purposes. The related requirement of disarmament which reduced Germany's great army to just 100,000 men and garrisoned the Rhine for 15 years was just as badly received, even though the provision had been cast as a prelude to general disarmament within Europe.

Ultimately the German government had no choice but to accept the broad terms of Versailles. However, many Germans saw this as capitulation, and conservatives, who wielded the country's economic power, dissociated themselves from government and from Republic. Disruptive as the terms of Versailles were, it was not they alone which sowed the seeds of the Hitler state, or set in motion the collapse of the new Republic. It was the way the Versailles Treaty polarised German political opinion between the mild socialists, democrats and Catholic centrists who shouldered the burden it imposed and the right-wing nationalists, the conservatives and the army who were revolted by it. And because the Weimar constitution was extremely democratic in form (for example, the system of proportional representation allowed the fullest possible value to all votes), there was little check to the consolidation of these antipathies. Even with hindsight, though, it is not fair to say that they led inexorably to the foundation of the Nazi state. That pathway required many more ingredients and dialectical forces before its course was clearly located.

I Part One

**Adolf Hitler
to 1919**

BERLIN

GERMANY

THE NETHERLANDS

1914-18 A soldier's existence at the front. Participated in set-piece battles; wounded and gassed; awarded military decorations.

August 1914 Hitler admitted as volunteer into the Bavarian Reserve Infantry Regiment - as dispatch runner. Regiment moved to Western Front October 1914.

1913 Hitler left Austria for Bavaria in order to avoid military service. Later arrested and extradited to Salzburg. Pleadings of poor health successfully prevented his conscription.

BELGIUM

1919 Hitler again in Munich. Given post in army political department for Bavaria. Later posted to Munich regiment as educational officer. Joins German Workers' Party, the forerunner of the NSDAP.

AUSTRIA-HUNGARY

Passau

Linz

1905-13 Hitler lived in Linz and then Vienna as a 'wanderer' without permanent employment. Twice tried unsuccessfully to enter Vienna art school. Supported financially by his family.

VIENNA

MUNICH
Braunau-am-Inn

Steyr
Lambach

SWITZERLAND

Born Austro-German border town, 1889, third of five children, three of whom died as infants. Father a civil servant. Family moved to Passau, inside Bavarian border, in 1892

1895 Hitler's father retired, taking his family to live on a homestead near Lambach.

1897 The Hitler family moved to Linz where Adolf Hitler attended grammar school until forced by poor results to transfer to school at Steyr.

Read anticlockwise

Fig. 1.1 Adolf Hitler, to 1919

The rise of the Nazi Party

3 *Adolf Hitler*

The story of how an obscure, Austrian-born corporal came to be dictator of Germany is one that will never cease to intrigue students of twentieth-century European history. Hitler's dictatorship was no ordinary one, either. It was founded upon the leader principle (*Führerprinzip*), whereby allegiance was sworn to the person of the leader rather than to any party or institution of state. The pattern was forcibly expressed in the salute: 'Heil Hitler!'. It found deeper manifestation in the semi-religious aura which increasingly surrounded Hitler as the Third Reich grew in strength. The cult of supreme leader was undoubtedly one to which Hitler himself aspired: his tactical manoeuvrings to take over leadership of the Nazi Party as early as 1921 are testament to this. But Hitler's authority had also to be rooted in a degree of mass acceptance by the German people. In effect, the two fed upon each other, which in itself helps to explain some of the energy and dynamism the Third Reich displayed in its albeit short existence.

It has been commonplace to search Hitler's early life for clues to the man as dictator. Hitler indulged in this himself when giving accounts of the formative influences upon his character and outlook, although there is as much fiction as fact in his autobiographical writing. Until his active involvement in politics in 1919 (Fig. 1.1), at the age of almost 30, two influences stand out as worthy of mention. Firstly, there were the years he spent in Vienna before the First World War – as a wanderer without permanent employment or trade. It was here that Hitler acquired the basic elements of what was to become his political ideology: nationalist, pan-German, anti-semitic, anti-marxist. They were derived from a combination of personal contacts and reading, typically devoid of any critical appraisal, and subsequently pursued with maniacal fervour. Secondly, there were the years Hitler spent in the German army during the First World War. In the view of many commentators, the discipline of war and the general order of military existence helped Hitler to translate his political ideas and dreamings into realistic, practical goals. The military model was to become the operational model for National Socialism.

4   *The Nazi Party: origins and early growth*

The Nazi Party originated from among the many nationalist, right-wing splinter groups which characterised the German-speaking political scene before and immediately following the First World War (Fig. 1.2). It began life as the German Workers' Party (DAP), but membership of the DAP was small and it was to be transformed after Hitler joined and became its propaganda officer. It was largely Hitler's tutelage that placed the Party on the political map – and under a new title: the National Socialist German Workers' Party (NSDAP).

Fig. 1.2 The genesis of the Nazi Party

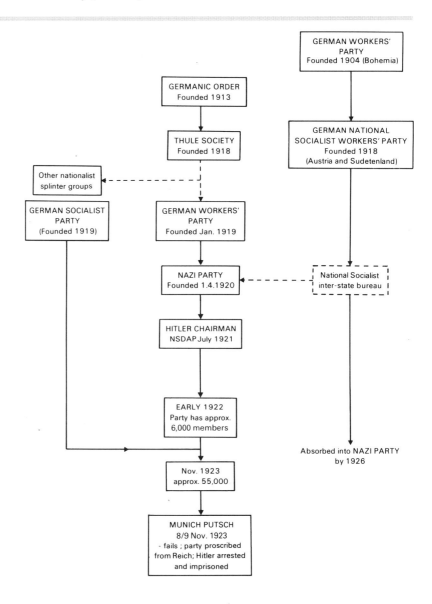

The DAP and the NSDAP also represented popular mass-appeal off-shoots of the Thule Society, a militant, nationalist, anti-semitic, anti-communist sect based in Munich. The sect had its own newspaper, the *Munich Observer*, and served as an important political and social arena for aspiring right-wing groups.

The early history of the Nazi Party is dominated by two themes: Hitler's drive to place the party under his own dictatorial control and the building up of a mass membership through radical reorganisation. Hitler was successful in both. He was Party leader by July 1921, with dictatorial powers. By 1923 membership had mushroomed with the entry of numerous ex-soldiers and free-corps members into the Party and with the absorption of other rightist groups. In the meantime, the Party had acquired the *Munich Observer* as its official newspaper, while Hitler's accomplice, Ernst Rohm, had established the formidable paramilitary wing of the NSDAP – the SA, or Stormtroopers (*Sturmabteilungen*).

In geographical terms, the singular feature of the early Nazi Party was its highly circumscribed focus. It began life in Munich and Munich remained the seat of its activity for almost a decade. The reasons for this were mainly twofold. Bavaria was a hotbed of political dissent with highly tolerant, 'reactional' city and state governments. Hitler insisted on the primacy of the Munich party organisation as a means of ensuring his dictatorial control. Both features tended to be reinforced by the tradition of German separatism. It would be wrong, though, to give the impression that the Nazi movement penetrated no further than southern Germany. The absorption in December 1922 of the German Socialist Party, which had local centres throughout much of Germany, widened Nazi influence almost overnight. Moreover, the symbolism of the party permeated an extensive area, emphasising what was to become a vital 'engine' in the acquisition of power: mass persuasion without real political understanding or conviction.

5 Mein Kampf

Most dictators have committed their ideas to paper to produce a universal testament in the biblical tradition. Hitler's testament was *Mein Kampf*. Part of it was written during his months in prison following the abortive *putsch*. It was published first in two volumes in 1925 and 1926. Later, a popular one-volume edition appeared which became the fundamental Nazi gospel. By the time of Hitler's death, over 8 million copies had been distributed or sold in Germany.

In its writing, *Mein Kampf* is turgid and disorganised; its terminology confused and inconsistent. As an exegesis of political ideology, it is both inept and unoriginal. For the enthusiast, however, none of these things mattered. That the book existed was enough. It lent a pseudo-intellectual respectability to Hitler in the popular imagination; it did not matter that thousands of copies lay unread and unopened.

For the more perceptive observer, *Mein Kampf* was undoubtedly an essential vehicle to the understanding of the Hitler mind. Some commentators saw it as a blueprint of what Germany was to become. Since 1945, it has been commonplace to deride the 'appeasement lobby' for failing to give adequate attention to the message *Mein Kampf* contains. But in both instances this is to ascribe to Hitler a rationality of thought and consistency of action which he patently lacked; and his foreign policy goals appeared totally incredible in the 1920s. *Mein Kampf* is important in revealing the range of ideas upon which Hitler drew and the overall frame in which those ideas were cast. It is especially instructive on Nazi propaganda techniques and on anti-semitism. Beyond this, it is the barest and loosest of guides to the Nazi regime as its course unfolded.

SOME OF THE INTELLECTUAL ROOTS OF MEIN KAMPF

Count Gobineau	nineteenth-century French racial theorist: the Aryan represented the pinnacle of racial purity.
H.S. Chamberlain	British-born writer on racism: saw race as key to history.
Hans Günther	German anthropologist, author of *Race history of the German nation*, 1992
Heinrich Treitschke	German professor of history who glorified the state and the necessity of war.
Richard Wagner	German romantic composer whose operas recalled the heroic myths of German culture.
Karl Haushofer	German professor of geopolitics: writer on the geographical bases of political power, including *Lebensraum* concept.

(Note: Hitler was probably conversant with few of the works of these figures first-hand. Ideas were invariably acquired second-hand from self-appointed Nazi ideologists and from the lowest of the popular press.)

THE IDEOLOGY OF NATIONAL SOCIALISM

HITLER'S VIEW OF HISTORY

He took a biological interpretation which saw history as a Darwinian struggle between races. Aryans formed the highest order and were the founders of culture. Jews were the lowest order and acted as destroyers of culture. Intermarriage was viewed as devilry and likely to debase the order of races. For the Aryan race to survive, its purity had to be preserved at all costs and its social dominance intensified.

GERMANY IN HITLER'S INTERPRETATION OF HISTORY

The German homeland and its people were seen as a receptive environment for the fulfilment of such a biological view of history, notably with its long-standing pockets of anti-semitism and its latent pan-German sentiments. As the German nation stood in the 1920s, it was beholden to liberalist and economic principles. The Nazi Party, with its substitution of leadership for liberal democracy and its realisation of the fundamental racial course of history, would arrest this pattern and set Germany on a path towards European and later world domination.

THE COURSE OF GERMAN REVIVAL AND SUPREMACY

The racist vision and its conjoining with the German nation state as defined at Versailles signalled an immediate quest for additional *Lebensraum* or 'living space'. The quest was given added urgency by the need to strike a stronger political bargaining position among the major European states. For Hitler, additional *Lebensraum* was to be found not in the nineteenth-century concept of empire but in extending the German state in Europe, in particular through a massive eastward colonisation of lands occupied by 'racially inferior' Slav and Latin peoples. Within such an expanded German homeland would emerge an elite international racial order to which all political, social and economic structures bowed and under which a progression of increasingly inferior racial groups laboured.

6   *Political ferment: 1923*

The year 1923 saw the fledgling Nazi Party at its zenith and at its nadir. The Party held its first national congress in Munich in January and membership rose rapidly to reach over 50,000 by November. That same month, however, witnessed the disastrous Munich *putsch* – an attempted *coup d'etat* by the Nazis which failed abysmally and led to Hitler's arrest and the banning of the Party from the entire Reich.

The dramatic turnabout in NSDAP fortunes was precipitated largely by outside events, for in 1923 the Weimar Republic was plagued by external and internal crises, presenting a tantalising seed-bed for dissenting political groups. In Bavaria, the seat of NSDAP political activity, the dissenting ground was rendered yet more fertile as a result of the highly equivocal attitude of its state government to that of the Reich and of the similarly disposed Bavarian *Reichswehr*.

From its inception, the Weimar government faced formidable problems, but the most outstanding was the issue of German reparations. In 1922, the

THE INFLATION		
Average monthly dollar quotations		
January	1919	8.9 marks
July	1919	14.0 ··
January	1920	64.8 ··
July	1920	39.5 ··
January	1921	64.9 ··
July	1921	76.7 ··
January	1922	191.8 ··
July	1922	493.2 ··
January	1923	17,972.0 ··
July	1923	353,412.0 ··
August	1923	4,620,455.0 ··
September	1923	98,860,000.0 ··
October	1923	25,260,208,000.0 ··
November 15	1923	4,200,000,000,000.0 marks

Source: Stolper, 1940

Fig. 1.3 The Inflation, 1919–23

Fig. 1.4 Political ferment: 1923

government of Chancellor Cuno requested a temporary suspension of reparations on account of the country's desperate economic plight. France refused the request and promptly occupied the Ruhr with troops. Cuno's government protested, refusing further co-operation over reparations, and stalemate prevailed. The Ruhr occupation and the passive resistance it generated spelt disaster for what little economic well-being remained in the Reich. Bankruptcy loomed, the value of the currency fell and resulted in rampant inflation (Fig. 1.3), while unrest erupted all over Germany.

In the Ruhr itself, separatist movements present since the collapse of the Wilhelmine state came rapidly to the surface (Fig 1.4). By late October, open clashes were occurring in Rhineland cities. Dissent in Bavaria gathered momentum in late September with the declaration of a state of emergency and in late October with the nullification of an earlier Bavarian decree putting the Law for the Protection of the Republic into effect. In Saxony and Thuringia, meanwhile, leftist movements had advanced sufficiently to be offered representation in their respective Land governments by mid-October. The Reich government's attempt to restore its authority by peaceful means met with little success. Moreover, at a time when the loyalty of the *Reichswehr* to the government was under strain from a conservative-monarchist conspiracy, the option of military force was less than automatic. But the communists in Saxony and Thuringia soon rescued the Reich government. By calling for resistance and violence against troops, they provided a clear excuse for the intervention of the *Reichswehr*, whereupon social democratic governments were quickly reinstated in both *Länder*. In Bavaria, though, where Hitler had already gained himself political leadership of the *Kampfbund* association of militant rightist groups, events soon developed their own momentum. At a nationalist meeting in a Munich beer hall on the evening of 8 November, attended by a host of senior state officials and military men, Hitler and his armed entourage burst in and declared the formation of a provisional Reich government. At first it seemed that the civil and military leaders had capitulated, but within 24 hours police and militia had defeated the *putschists*. The organisation of the *coup* had been inept: for instance, vital communication offices were left untouched; but more significant was the tenuous unity of the Bavarian right – Hitler intent upon personal dictatorship while others sought restoration of the Bavarian monarchy.

7   *The parliamentary route to power*

Just 13 months after the Munich *putsch*, Hitler obtained his release from Landsberg gaol only to find the remnants of his political party in chronic disarray. The tenuous bonds between the local party groups across Germany were quickly split by the failed *putsch* and separatist tendencies soon appeared. In Bavaria, the support which Hitler had received from the 'establishment' was quickly dissipated following the events of November 1923 and right-wing opinion there became even more sharply polarised than in the earlier years of the Nazi Party.

Fig. 1.5 Electoral districts

Electoral districts

1. East Prussia	19. Hesse-Nassau
2. Berlin	20. Cologne-Aachen
3. Potsdam II	21. Koblenz-Trier
4. Potsdam I	22. Düsseldorf-East
5. Frankfurt a.d. Oder	23. Düsseldorf-West
6. Pomerania	24. Upper Bavaria-Swabia
7. Breslau	25. Lower Bavaria
8. Liegnitz	26. Franconia
9. Oppeln	27. Palatinate
10. Magdeburg	28. Dresden-Bautzen
11. Merseburg	29. Leipzig
12. Thuringia	30. Chemnitz-Zwickau
13. Schleswig-Holstein	31. Württemberg
14. Weser-Ems	32. Baden
15. East Hanover	33. Hesse-Darmstadt
16. South Hanover-Brunswick	34. Hamburg
17. Westphalia-North	35. Mecklenburg
18. Westphalia-South	

The grand lesson of the failed *putsch* was that any Nazi revolution would have to be organised through the existing machinery of government and politics (Fig. 1.5). To many of the Nazi Party faithful, a campaign for parliamentary representation appeared anathema, but Hitler and several of his closest advisers quickly recognised that there was little alternative and thus the Party made its first foray into nationwide legal representation with the Reichstag elections of May 1924 (Fig. 1.6). Given the events of the preceding November, the results were surprisingly favourable. The radical right in combination achieved 32 Reichstag seats and 6.5 per cent of the national vote. In Mecklenburg and Franconia, they registered results of over 20 per cent. There were further Reichstag elections in December 1924. This time, however, the radical right fared badly. Their seats fell to 14 and their percentage national vote to 3. Regionally, only Mecklenburg survived as a significant focus of support. This was the beginning of almost six years in the political wilderness. In the Reichstag elections of May 1928, for example, the Party's percentage share of the national vote fell to 2.6 and there was not a single electoral district in which it polled above 10 per cent. The victors of the election were the Social Democrats, who were able to form a majority coalition government. The communists also gained ground, taking just over 10 per cent of the national vote.

Electoral breakthrough

The relative impotence of the Nazi Party as an electoral force in the later 1920s was largely explained by the growing stability of Weimar Germany. The apparent success of Foreign Minister Stresemann in handling the reparations issue, for example, and increasing economic vitality at home ran counter to the appeal of National Socialism and radical right-wing sentiments generally. However, the pattern did not last. By early 1929, signs of weakness in the world economy were becoming plain and the crash of the New York stock market in October finally set the seal on an unprecedented worldwide slump. Germany, with its post-war economy so dependent on

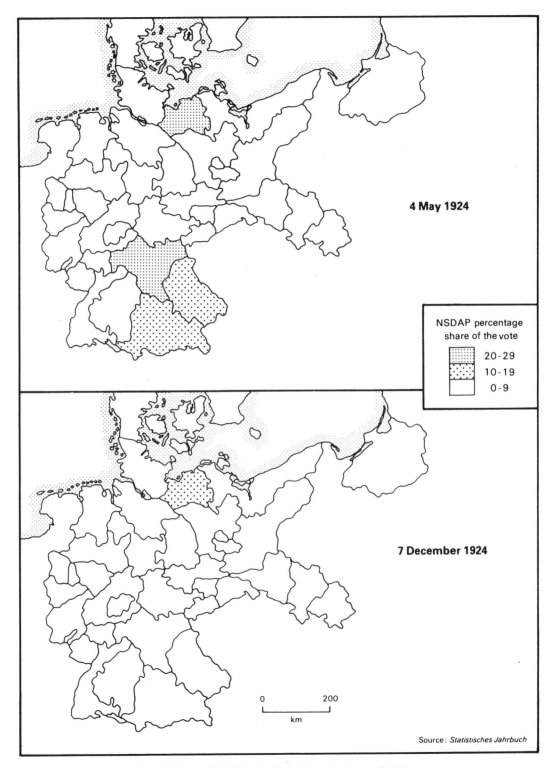

Fig. 1.6 The NSDAP in the Reichstag elections of 1924

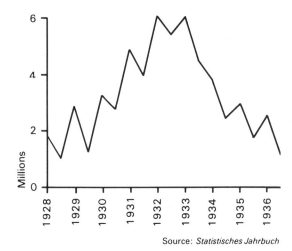

Source: *Statistisches Jahrbuch*

Source: *Statistisches Jahrbuch*

Fig. 1.7 (top left) Volume of external trade, 1928–36 (billion RM at 1928 prices)

Fig. 1.8 (top right) Unemployment, 1928–36 (January and July totals)

Fig. 1.9 (right) Landtag elections, 1928–30: NSDAP/Völk Nat. bloc percentage share of vote

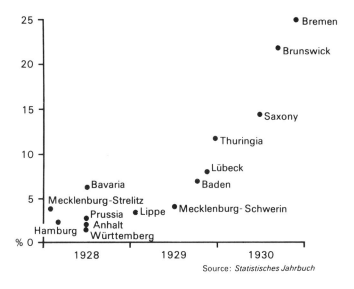

Source: *Statistisches Jahrbuch*

foreign investment, suffered very badly (Figs 1.7 and 1.8). Parallel to this, a separate political ferment had been growing at home over Stresemann's negotiations for a final agreement over reparations. The right-wing parties had combined to campaign for a national plebiscite on the question. The Nazis joined in this and quickly found their access to the political arena much enlarged. Although the plebiscite, when it came in 1929, resulted in a decisive defeat for the right, this was incidental to the more general remobilisation of right-wing sympathies which the campaign set in train. The pattern was clearly expressed in the various state elections of 1929 where the Nazis again began to register poll shares of the order of 10 and 20 per cent (Fig. 1.9). It showed itself still more clearly in the Reichstag elections of September 1930 when the Party secured 18.3 per cent of the national vote

Fig. 1.10 Reichstag elections, 14 September 1930

and 107 seats (Fig. 1.10). Party support had become generalised at 20 to 30 per cent across much of the North German Plain and the south-east, except for cities and industrial foci. Representation was weaker in the Catholic south and the west, including Bavaria, but no district failed to register gains in Nazi support alongside the corresponding votes of May 1928 and December 1924.

The Nazi Party (NSDAP)

Few political parties attract representation from all sections of the community in uniform measure (Fig. 1.11). As an extremist party, the NSDAP predictably found far stronger support in some sections than in others, although few of these conformed to the familiarly accepted breeding grounds of political radicalism. The Party found most of its members from among the diverse ranks of the middle class, especially among the *petit bourgeoisie*. For example, self-employed farmers, artisans and tradesmen were represented in almost double the proportion suggested by the national breakdown of occupational groups. Much the same was true of the free professions, the civil service and white-collar workers generally. Working-class groups, however, were equivalently under-represented. The middle

Fig. 1.11 The social characteristics of the NSDAP membership

The occupational structure of the NSDAP membership by the outbreak of the depression

The occupational structure of the NSDAP membership compared with the national occupational structure as of the Reich census of 1925

The age structure of NSDAP recruits, 1925–32, measured against the age structure of the Reich population

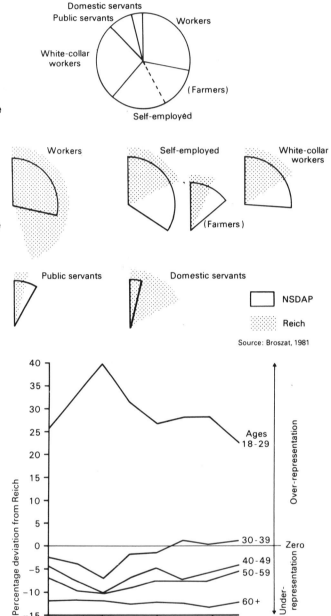

class were attracted to join the Party not for the vision of society that it embraced (this vision was vague, anyway), but for its stand against various elements of the established order. In the most immediate sense, that order was represented by the Weimar regime. Among the traditional middle-class, especially the pre-war generation, the democratisation launched under Weimar had undermined a status already under threat through the social forces of industrialism. For the beneficiaries of industrialism, that is the *new*

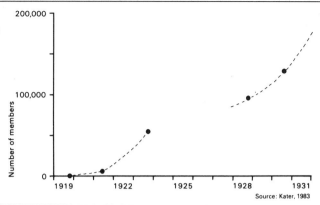

Fig. 1.12 NSDAP membership, 1919–30

Source: Kater, 1983

middle class, Weimar was associated with economic failure and insecurity of employment, regardless of the way in which such features had as much to do with the workings of modern capitalism as they did to any particular political system.

Aside from its class bias, the other striking feature of the 'adolescent' NSDAP was the youth of its membership. In part, this was the result of deliberate Party policy: young, immature minds were correctly perceived as more receptive to propaganda techniques; it would have been much more difficult to achieve the same levels of persuasion among those with longer political and constitutional perspectives. However, the whole style of the Nazi Party was one that was likely to appeal to the physical and social energies of youth. The rite of the mass meeting, the adventurism of the paramilitary SA, the camaraderie of the Hitler Youth with its emphasis on physical training, and the *naïveté* and violent apocalyptic romanticism of the movement – all these features (and many others) set the NSDAP apart from the traditional political parties, except the communists. As unemployment rose in the Depression, therefore, and as the hatreds and fears of the NSDAP spread like a contagious disease, the youthful following acquired a secular momentum from which the Party organs fed easily as much as they manipulated (Fig. 1.12).

The NSDAP's appeal within the wider electoral community may be understood in terms of the way it sought to rediscover the practices and spirit of the national community (*Volksgemeinschaft*). The divisions of society were to be erased; security and normality restored. It is in this sense that one can begin to comprehend the Party's nihilism. It was anti-semitic, anti-marxist and anti-capitalist, but there was a measure in which these oppositions and hatreds were labels that were readily interchanged. Moreover, almost any political party which stood even remotely against the modern industrial ethos would have found a ripe body of support in Germany during the years of the Depression. In fact, alternative political parties were in some respects appraised less for their professed ideologies than for the socio-economic dispositions of their primary supporters. Thus were socialists and communists viewed by Hitler as agents of modern capitalist industry. A related outcome was that even the most disparate interests came to be unified behind Nazism.

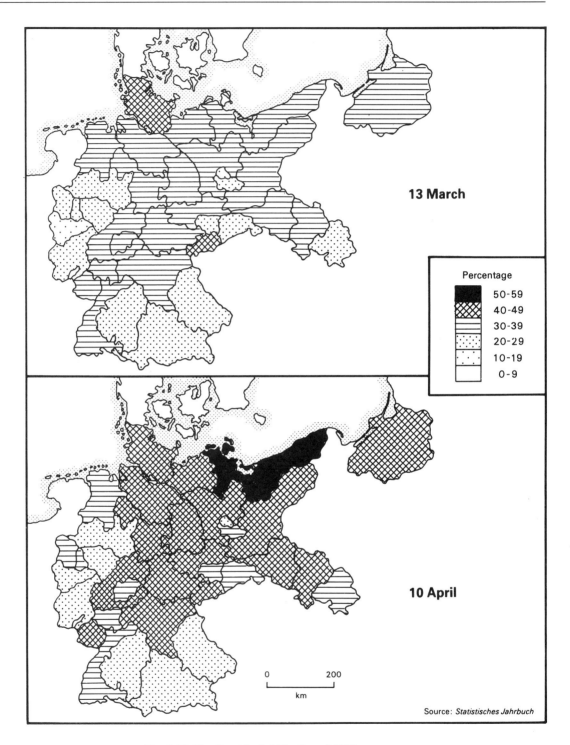

Fig. 1.13 The Presidential Election of 1932.
Percentage of votes cast for Hitler

Hitler's candidature for the presidency: spring 1932

Hindenburg's term of office as Reich President expired in the spring of 1932 and the prospect quickly became the focus for a round of intense political manoeuvring among the different forces of opposition and Brüning's emergency government. Hitler looked towards leadership in government if his party was to agree to support Brüning's scheme to re-elect Hindenburg. This proved too bitter a pill for Hindenburg and his allies to swallow. The outcome was thus a contested election in which Hitler soon emerged as Hindenburg's major rival, readily eclipsing the Nationalists' candidate, Düsterberg. The result of the first contest on 13 March revealed a staggering advance in the National Socialist vote against that of the September 1930 Reichstag elections. It rose from just under 6.5 million to just under 11.5 million, forming 30.1 per cent of the total. Moreover, this support was general throughout northern, eastern and central Germany. Hindenburg polled some 18.6 million votes but just failed to secure an absolute majority (Fig. 1.13). Thus a second election resulted in which the ageing President obtained the necessary majority, but where Hitler increased his share of the vote to 36.8 per cent (Fig. 1.14). The additional Nazi support came almost entirely from the areas which showed most strongly in favour of Hitler in the first election contest. A key to understanding the scale of Nazi success was the frenetic nature of the election campaign, which was masterminded by Goebbels. The Party machine sought to penetrate every quarter of Germany and, in a novel propaganda *coup*, Hitler travelled by aeroplane from one election rally to another.

Fig. 1.14 Votes cast for the two main Presidential contenders

Source: *Statistisches Jahrbuch*

Fig. 1.15 Reichstag elections, 14 September 1930 and 31 July 1932

Electoral domination

The crowning point of the Nazis' electoral success came in the Reichstag elections of 31 July 1932. They increased their Reichstag seats from 107 to 230 and acquired 13.7 million popular votes. From the accompanying maps (Fig. 1.15), it can be seen that Party support had become yet more clearly generalised throughout northern, eastern and central Germany. Whereas in September 1930, its strongest support was spread disparately across the face of the country, by July 1932 it was continuous over extensive land areas. Only the predominantly Catholic south and west had resisted the appeals of National Socialism. With 37 per cent of the popular vote, the Nazis easily outstripped their former winning rival, the Social Democrats (Fig. 1.16). Theoretically, Hitler was in a position to lead a coalition government. It was also possible that he might be drawn into a coalition under the then chancellor, von Papen. Neither scheme materialised, however. The President held Hitler and his Party in distaste and would not countenance Hitler as chancellor or in any other prominent cabinet position. The prospect of a Hitler coalition, meanwhile, evaporated when Chancellor von Papen obtained a presidential decree for dissolving the Reichstag before it had even sat.

The new Reichstag elections on 6 November 1932 saw the Nazis lose

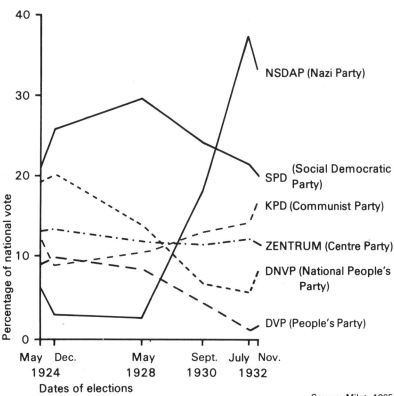

Fig. 1.16 Share of popular vote of main political parties, 1924–32

Source: Milatz 1965

Fig. 1.17 Reichstag elections,
6 November 1932

Reichstag elections
6 November 1932

Reduction of NSDAP share
of vote against elections of
31 July 1932

6-8 percentage points

3-5 percentage points

<3 percentage points

Source: *Statistisches Jahrbuch*

ground on a significant scale (Fig. 1.17). Their seats fell from 230 to 196 and their share of the popular vote from 37 to 33 per cent. Accompanying this, divisions were appearing in the Party as a result of the frustrations experienced in achieving power by popular consent. Paradoxically, however, the waning Nazi vote and the internal unrest were two of the very factors which propelled Hitler to the chancellorship. By the end of January 1933, President Hindenburg had agreed to a government led by Hitler, the cabinet consisting of eight conservatives and only three Nazis.

8   *The road to dictatorship*

Although the Nazis failed to obtain a majority share of the popular vote in each of the elections of 1932, they undoubtedly held a fairly strong mandate to govern given the complex system of proportional representation of the Weimar constitution. But Hitler's chancellorship, together with the two supporting Nazi members of cabinet, did not really derive from this mandate. It sprang first from the presidency but, behind the façade of that office, from a variety of power blocks (Fig. 1.19) which had long been active in German political life and which had been gathering momentum in the economic and political turmoil which characterised Weimar Germany from 1929. Since March 1930, in fact, the authority of the Reichstag as the institutional embodiment of popular political opinion and as the forum of national government had been in a state of semi-abeyance. The collapse of the Social Democrat coalition in spring 1930 marked the beginning of an era of extra-parliamentary government under Article 48 of the Weimar constitution. The original purpose of this constitutional provision was to give the presidency special powers in times of national emergency. By mid-1930, the provision was being used to bypass the authority of the Reichstag. The Reichstag itself could repeal all legislation under such emergency rule, but since the presidency had power to dissolve the Reichstag, this was a poor

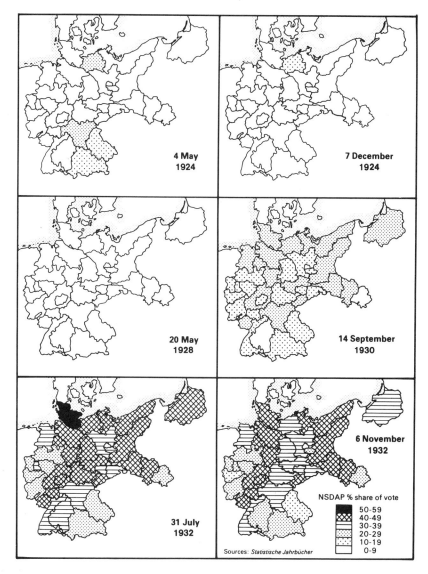

Fig. 1.18 The electoral performance of the Nazi Party, 1924–32

4 May
1924

7 December
1924

20 May
1928

14 September
1930

31 July
1932

6 November
1932

NSDAP % share of vote

50-59
40-49
30-39
20-29
10-19
0-9

Sources: *Statistische Jahrbücher*

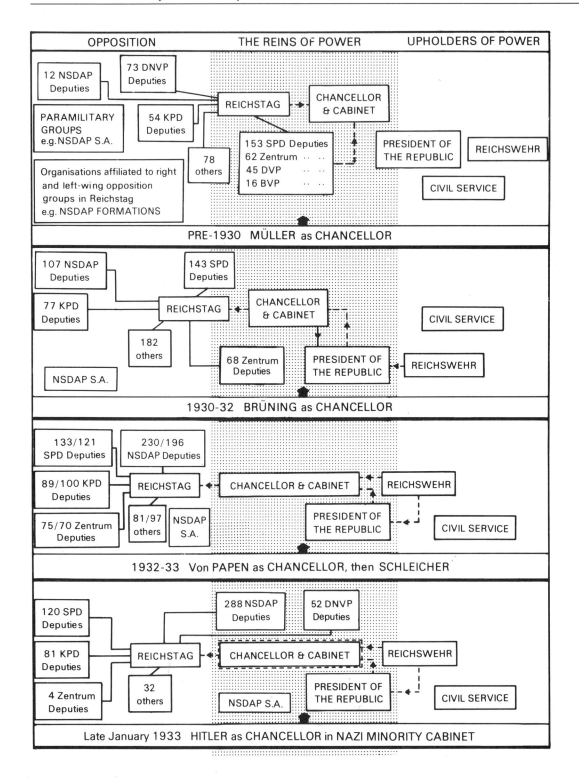

Fig. 1.19 The road to dictatorship

safeguard. The pattern was set in motion when President Hindenburg appointed Heinrich Brüning to the chancellorship without the Reichstag's consent and threatened to invoke emergency rule if Brüning's policies were blocked. In July 1930, the Reichstag duly threw out Brüning's plans and a dissolution decree followed. The position was by no means irretrievable, since a newly elected Reichstag might have been more amenable to the new chancellor's plans. However, the September Reichstag elections saw strong gains for the extremist parties. The result was a polarisation of the pattern. Between 1930 and 1932, the German President ratified 109 emergency decrees while the Reichstag passed just 29 bills, nearly all of them minor. By June 1932, the Reichstag's status had been reduced to that of a rump, its views neither listened to nor sought.

This was the framework of power relations in which Hitler first acceded to government. The framework is important in making clear that the Nazis did not come to power with the consent of the Reichstag, the parliamentary road, however far along that way they progressed. But it is even more vitally important in understanding the speed with which Hitler was able to move towards the creation of a more authoritarian and totalitarian regime. In the latter aspect, Hitler's actions were presaged by one of his immediate predecessors as chancellor: Franz von Papen. In mid-July 1932, von Papen instituted a peaceful *coup d'etat* over the Prussian Land administration in an attempt to consolidate his shaky power base. The government there readily capitulated and the result was the undermining of a critical element of German federalism. The incorporation of Prussia was achieved through an emergency presidential decree. Hitler enjoyed the same facility upon his assumption of office in late January 1933.

Extra-parliamentary government presents a route to dictatorship which can be readily elucidated. It hardly explains why the route ended in a Nazi takeover. The Party's electoral successes were undoubtedly substantial; and to an extent which transcended the impotence of the Reichstag. But the final clues to Nazi accession lie in simple historical eventuation. The Nazis' mild reverse in the November 1932 polls which gave their opponents a false sense of confidence, army responsiveness to Nazi schemes of re-armament, the authoritarian designs of Hindenburg and von Papen, and the acquiescence of big business were some of the elements which in complex combination eventually placed Hitler in power. With a backcloth composed of the economic and social cataclysms of the Depression, the Nazi entourage entered upon a predisposed stage-set, its choreography determined largely by the actions of others, to emerge with lightning speed into the most infamous police state of the twentieth century.

9   *The* Führerprinzip

When examining the growth and organisation of the Nazi Party and, after 1933, the workings of the Nazi state, it is difficult to erase from the mind such common organisational principles as delegation and hierarchy. But one has to do this in order to understand fully the operation of the Nazi machine.

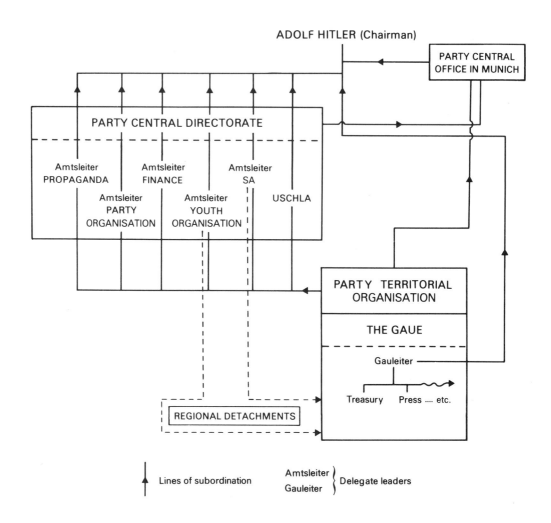

Fig. 1.20 The *Führerprinzip*: Party organisation (circa 1926)

Despite their advancing scale and intricacy, the institutions of Nazism bore no shred of comparison with orthodox systems of administrative bureaucracy. The *Führerprinzip* placed individual personages above bureaucratic structures as the final authority. The result was that Nazi leaders could interfere at every level, at will or whim. The only power relationship recognised within the *Führerprinzip* was the responsibility of subordinates to their superiors. This relationship was undefined and yet total. The pattern was already well established in the mid-1920s, as the accompanying chart of Party organisation reveals (Fig. 1.20). Despite the façade of an administrative hierarchy involving delegation of authority, the reality was otherwise. The Gauleiters, for instance, could exploit their regional bases to a degree quite inconsistent with the position of their offices in an orthodox administrative system. They were directly subservient to Hitler (by whom they were appointed), and saw themselves as his direct agents in the field. However, other Nazi leaders viewed the Gauleiters as their own subordinates. One of these was the Chief of Central Party Office; another the *Amtsleiter* for Party Finance. The inevitable result was a remarkable confusion of responsibility, one that became a hallmark of Nazism. The *Führerprinzip* became a pervasive feature of the Party and, later, of the state. While Hitler represented its ultimate embodiment, surrogate leadership became widespread in the Third Reich. It was a crucial symptom of the style of Hitler's dictatorship: improvised, remote from details, and built on patronage not principle.

10   *The Third Reich is born*

In the eyes of many outside the Nazi Party, Hitler's chancellorship was a temporary expedient in a time of difficult political and constitutional transition. Few opponents of the National Socialists were unaware of the extra-legal activities of organisations such as the SA, but most saw this as a necessary evil given Hitler's mass following and most were complacent about the opposition's ability to control the Nazis' course, whether through the federal structure or via one of the major institutions of state. That an institution like the *Reichswehr* should give token backing to Hitler reinforced this state of mind, for here was the ultimate guardian (historically) of Reich security. These features combined to give a muted character to the forces of opposition as the authoritarian and totalitarian goals of the Nazis were rapidly revealed. And before more concerted efforts could be set in train, the Nazis had all but destroyed the legitimate means of dissent. One of the critical difficulties faced by opposition groups was the astonishing speed with which Hitler was able to consolidate the Nazis' power. In part this was a result of preceding developments: the suspension of parliamentary government and its replacement by government by emergency decree; and the absorption of Prussia into the Reich. Hitler capitalised fully on the emergency powers at his disposal as chancellor and, by managing to invest his two cabinet members as Ministers of the Interior in the Reich and in Prussia, the Nazis held a trump card in their ability to manipulate the rule of law very quickly. However, none of this can detract from the simple fact that the Nazis had a powerful grass-roots Party organisation, highly effective coercive forces (the SA and the SS) with which their will could be reinforced and, above all, a leader and central Party apparatus with a clearly defined goal which was to be pursued with unremitting zeal and sometimes acute political acumen.

Hitler's first move as chancellor was to obtain a decree for the dissolution of the Reichstag and the calling of new elections on 5 March 1933. If the Nazis could be seen to win a parliamentray mandate, the task of political and constitutional manipulation would be that much easier. The dissolution was quickly followed by a decree giving power to ban public meetings and the press where they were deemed to undermine the security of the Reich. In

---

MINISTERIAL CONTINUITY, 1932–33

Von PAPEN Cabinet 1932	SCHLEICHER Cabinet 1932/3	HITLER Cabinet 30 Jan. 1933
		Hitler
Von Papen		VonPapen (Vice-Chancellor)
Von Neurath	Von Neurath	Von Neurath (Foreign Office)
Krosigk	Krosigk	Krosigk (Finance)
	Von Rübenach	Von Rübenach (Communications)
Gürtner	Gürtner	Gürtner (Justice)
		Seldte
		Hugenberg
		Frick
		Goering
		Von Blomberg

THE ARENA FOR THE MAKING OF AN AUTHORITARIAN NAZI STATE

The forces against authoritarianism	*The forces in favour of authoritarianism in some form*
Political parties: KPD (including Communists' Combat League)	President
SPD (including Reichsbanner organisation)	Reichswehr Non-Nazi cabinet members
Free Trade Unions	Political parties DNVP Zentrum DVP
Reichstag officers	
Legal system and the Weimar constitution	Civil service, especially ministerial bureaucracy in Reich, in Prussia, and in some Länder
	{ 'Big Business { Reich Association of German Industry
	Reich Land League
	Stahlhelm

effect, this became a blanket facility for silencing opposition in the run-up to the election and was most successfully applied in Prussia under Goering's interior ministryship and in those remaining *Länder* where National Socialist governments prevailed. Von Papen's Prussian *coup* of July 1932 had not entirely taken over the reins of administration and control, but this was completed in a presidential decree of 6 February 1933, whereupon police chiefs and other officials unsympathetic to the Nazi cause were replaced. The spreading tentacles of Nazi control in Prussia gathered further momentum when on 22 February Goering set up an auxiliary police force drawn from the ranks of the SA, the SS and the *Stahlhelm*, ostensibly to combat the excesses of political opposition. The relative moderation which characterised the Nazis' approach to their opponents in Hitler's first month of power was brought to a dramatic close when the Dutch communist van der Lubbe set fire to the Reichstag building on 27 February 1933. It was the

Fig. 1.21 Reichstag elections, 5 March 1933

act of an individual, but the Nazis seized upon it as indicating a general communist uprising and draconian measures were demanded. By the Reichstag Fire Decree of the following day, all basic democratic rights enjoyed under the Weimar constitution were terminated and the Reich government was accorded special powers to override the Land governments in the event of their failing to observe the decree adequately. In Prussia, Goering did not hesitate to use the decree to make large-scale arrests of communists and any persons who co-operated with or supported them. Outside Prussia, arrests were more selective, but all German Communist Party (KPD) activities became illegal.

In the Reichstag elections of 5 March 1933, the Nazi Party polled 43.9 per cent of the national vote, an increase of almost 11 percentage points over the previous November election (Fig. 1.21). Even given the impediments to a free election posed by the various emergency decrees of February 1933, this result constituted one of the strongest mandates in the electoral history of the Weimar Republic. And the degree to which a free election was impeded is counterbalanced by the extraordinary 88.7 per cent turnout, the more so given that the election was the third inside a year. In the preceding votes of July and November 1932, the turnouts had been 84 and 80 per cent respectively. Previous non-voters were clearly being mobilised and, judging from the increase in Nazi support, Hitler's appeal was a decisive influence in their political activation. The Nazi election performance was not, however, sufficient to achieve a parliamentary majority. Hitler achieved this only through the indulgence of the DNVP, which gave him 51.9 per cent of the popular vote in total.

It is clear from the electoral map that the Nazis did not enjoy overwhelming support anywhere. They remained strongest in East Prussia, in the eastern border lands and in the north, but in none of the Reichstag electoral districts did they record more than 56 per cent of the vote. In the industrial west, meanwhile, the Nazis were supported by less than 40 per cent of voters.

Hitler interpreted the election results as a grand success, as a mandate for 'national revolution'. And as the following weeks and months of 1933 unfolded, this view was put vigorously into practice. Now Hitler began to make use of the elaborate Party organisation on the ground, including the SA and the SS. The paramilitary wings moved swiftly into action in those *Länder* where the Party still had no majority, namely in Bavaria, Baden, Hesse, Saxony and Württemberg, and in the city states of Hamburg, Bremen and Lübeck (Fig. 1.22). In many cases, their precipitateness was self-appointed, Hitler playing no direct executive role. To this extent, Germany was seeing the beginnings of a revolution from below. Town halls, courts, banks, trade union, political party and newspaper offices were occupied. There were summary arrests of opponents of the regime (Fig. 1.23). The setting up of auxiliary police forces, as had occurred earlier in Prussia, proliferated, and the subordination of these police groupings to the regular state police (and hence to the Reich government) became increasingly suspect. What Goering had already achieved in Prussia was now repeated even more rigorously in what remained of the federal state. In a matter of days, in fact, effective government of the Länder was in the hands of Reich Commissioners, many of them prominent Nazi officials. The strongest resistance came in Bavaria, but the Nazis won the day when appeals for the intervention of the *Reichswehr* were rebuffed by Hindenburg, the Reich President.

With the reins of government at regional as well as national level in his hands, Hitler set about strengthening his role as chancellor. He did this first by persuading the new Reichstag to grant him (as chancellor) full executive and legislative powers for a period of four years. This the Reichstag did on 23 March 1933, after the Nazis had locked up the 81 KPD deputies and won over the Catholic Centre Party with vague promises in order to get the required two-thirds majority. The second stage was the progressive elimination of the parties. The parties of the left, the communists especially, were already well on the way to extinction as a result of the Reichstag Fire Decree. By late May, all communist assets had been seized by law. A month later the same threat met the SPD and that party was also prohibited from further political activity. The remaining political parties all gradually dissolved themselves. Some of their members saw alliance with the Nazis as the only way ahead; some gave in after persistent political manoeuvring and intimidation by the Nazis; others, like those making up the Catholic Centre Party, were won over by clever propaganda moves – in this instance largely by the conclusion of a concordat between the Nazi government and Rome, the Catholic Church having previously set its face against Nazism. The

The last bastions of the republic

- Länder not controlled by NSDAP, early March 1933
- City states not controlled by NSDAP
- Prussia (under NSDAP control)
- Länder under NSDAP control
- –·–·– International boundary

Fig. 1.22 The last bastions of the republic

Source: Broszat, 1968

Fig. 1.23 Numbers detained in concentration camps, 31 July 1933

Centre Party was the last to go, and within days of its dissolution, ironically on 14 July, a law was enacted prohibiting the establishment of political parties. The NSDAP became the only political party. The one-party state was born, with Hitler as its leader.

The monopoly of political power and the subjugation of Prussian autonomy and that of the remaining Länder could not, of course, deliver an authoritarian, totalitarian Nazi state overnight. To wipe out one's competitors for power was one thing, but to dismantle all the elements and vestiges of a pluralist republic, a federal republic at that, was further away. The Civil Service was purged of Jews and political unreliables under an Act of April 1933, but steps had at the same time to be taken to preserve the Civil Service from over-zealous Nazi infiltration for fear of general administrative impotence. The working classes remained a potential threat to Nazism, particularly through their trade union organisations. Thus Hitler was driven again into clever propaganda frays which led to the banning of free unions on 2 May 1933 and the enrolment of all employees in the German Labour Front (*Deutsche Arbeitsfront* – DAF), a kind of single national union. Any ideas that the DAF would have real independent bargaining power quickly proved illusory, however; Hitler, in alliance with the leaders of big business, ensured against this. In most cases of this kind, it was largely a matter of political will and expediency, and time, before the bulk of the substructures of Weimar and Wilhelmine Germany had been swept away. Much more problematic, however, were the conflicts which were emerging within the National Socialist camp itself, in large part deriving from the *Führerprinzip*. The most serious came to a head in 1934. It concerned the position of the SA and Röhm in the new National Socialist state.

11   *The Stormtroopers*

The SA or *Sturmabteilungen* (Stormtroopers) were the strong-arm squad of the Nazi Party and they grew very much in line with it. Ernst Röhm, later to become SA leader, joined the German Workers' Party even before Hitler and was soon recruiting old members of the *Freikorps* and ex-servicemen to swell the ranks of the new Nazi Party, by then under Hitler's tutelage. From its very beginnings, the SA became an instigator of political violence. It was a protection squad for party members and their activities, but, much more than this, it actively sought confrontation with other political groupings, especially of the left. In this way the party was propelled into the centre of the public arena whether the public was interested or not. And because the Bavarian authorities harboured strong right-wing sympathies, acts of political violence perpetrated by the SA were viewed with remarkable complacency.

With the failure of the Munich *putsch*, the SA followed the party into relative obscurity, although not without a festering dispute concerning the SA as a militaristic organisation. SA leaders saw their organisation as revolutionary and insurgent. Hitler wished for subservience to the political leadership, eschewing the idea of a military role.

As the Nazi Party regrouped in the later 1920s, so too did the SA.

Fig. 1.24 The size of the SA in the Eastern Prussian provinces 1931–32

The eastern provinces proved especially fertile ground for SA recruitment as the Depression intensified. Not only was there growing unemployment in the industrial districts of Silesia, but rising *underemployment* in farming areas. In Königsberg in East Prussia, in June 1931, 35 per cent of SA members were actually farmers.

Recruitment increased among young people, notably in working-class urban areas where marches and demonstrations, invariably ending in street brawls, soon became almost nightly events. From being largely an old fighters' organisation, the SA was becoming an outlet for the frustrated energies of youth, a pattern that intensified as unemployment climbed during the Depression years. As an exclusively male organisation, the mob violence of the SA became a kind of virility test. And whatever else, SA membership gave a uniform, food and a sense of belonging where before there had often been none.

Statistics about SA membership are problematic. The turnover rate of

Gaue showing highest dismissals,
1934-5

		(% dismissed)
I	Cologne-Aachen	32.4
II	North Westphalia	35.1
III	Kurhessen	30.0
IV	Hesse-Nassau	32.8
V	Swabia	35.1
VI	East Hanover	24.0
VII	Pomerania	31.6
VIII	East Prussia	32.1

Source: Orlow, 1973

Fig. 1.25 The purge of party leaders

membership was high. Some members were extraordinarily active, but many were not. Most people joined for opportunistic reasons rather than from any deep political commitment to the Nazi movement. Before Röhm took over as SA chief in January 1931, membership was roughly 100,000. Under his organising energy, there was a striking expansion of membership (Fig. 1.24) and a consolidation of SA territorial organisation. By early 1932, there were nearly 300,000 members and the SA had been transformed into the most efficient of party armies, with an elaborate central command organisation and 21 regional groups.

As the Nazi Party's fortunes at the polls improved over 1930 and 1932, SA leaders increasingly perceived their organisation as poised for a new Nazi *putsch* and, more widely, as the imminent purveyors of a social revolution. For Hitler, this proved both a blessing and a threat. The latent force represented by the SA and the more immediate street violence were obvious bargaining levers in the disintegrating face of the Weimar Republic.

But the danger was in over-hasty action which could summarily prejudice the Party's goals. By a combination of luck and judgement, Hitler and the Party leadership successfully walked this tightrope, even with a temporary ban on the SA in mid-1932 as a consequence of government anxiety over a *coup*.

Hitler's accession to the chancellorship saw people flocking to join the SA and by 1934 membership may have been approaching 3 million. SA intimidation and street violence reached a new pitch throughout the spring and summer of 1933 and were instrumental in deterring the limited forces of opposition to Nazism that remained. The SA officer corps lived in feverish expectation of taking a leading part in Nazi government and in a revolutionary dismantling of the existing state. However, reality proved otherwise. Hitler consolidated Nazi power with the co-operation and connivance of the traditional German elites. Official positions went not to old stalwarts but to converts from the German establishment. The resulting tension was inevitable and culminated in a bloody purge of SA leaders in mid-summer 1934, including the murder of Röhm (Fig. 1.25). Subsequently, the SA was entirely restructured to make it into a kind of training ground for the Wehrmacht. It became a subservient organisation, stripped of its former trappings of power. The SA had performed a vital task in the political warfare leading up to January 1933. Thereafter it became dispensable. Nazi Party leaders who were active in the SA, or in close sympathy with it, were removed in a series of purges over 1934–5, as the map above demonstrates.

II Part Two

Administrative and political structure

The Nazi state defies most conventions of understanding and explanation. It embraced no clear constitution; indeed, the constitution of Weimar was never formally abolished. Its relationship with the Party was never clearly defined. The process whereby all legislative and executive power came to rest in Hitler's hands displays no thread of legality. The most meaningful label for the Third Reich is the *Hitler state*. If it had a constitution, it was represented in the will of the Führer, Adolf Hitler. This will formed a supreme authority which was inalienable and unlimited. If one seeks to rationalise the Nazi state, it is thus to Hitler that one turns. But this presupposes that rationality was a prevailing feature of the Hitler mind: it was not. One has also to confront the facility with which Hitler delegated his power, as well as the ability of delegate leaders to make laws under the guise of carrying out the Führer's will.

In the early days of the Third Reich, government was by a collegiate body, the cabinet, and the continued existence of the presidency (still occupied by the ageing Hindenburg) maintained a basic element of the constitutional state (Fig. 2.1). But this pattern did not last long. Within months of his accession as chancellor, Hitler had achieved a position of absolute authority in cabinet, by deviousness and personal popularity. Subsequently, meetings of the cabinet became fewer and fewer, its role reduced to that of an advisory council; indeed, after February 1938 it ceased to function altogether. The office of President effectively disappeared when Hindenburg died in August 1934; Hitler united it with the chancellorship, but nevertheless assumed all the presidency's powers, including supreme command of the armed forces. Henceforward, Hitler was designated Führer and Reich Chancellor. The Reichstag, the other major organ of legal authority, had witnessed a progressive erosion of its power even before Hitler's chancellorship. The action against communists of late February 1933, following the Reichstag fire, weakened it further. Then, under the Enabling Law of 23 March 1933, it was largely emasculated. It remained as an institution, but simply to acclaim the laws and practices of National Socialism.

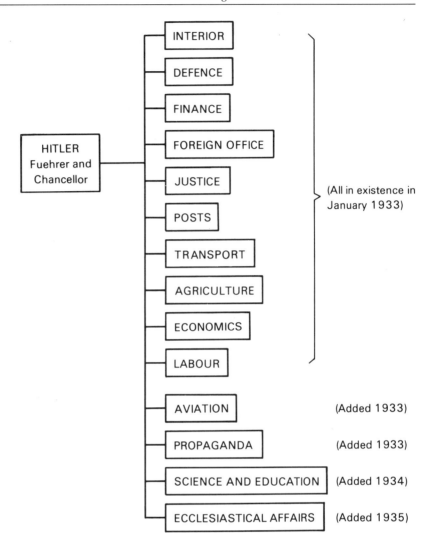

Fig. 2.1 The Ministries of the Nazi State circa 1936

INTERIOR

DEFENCE

FINANCE

FOREIGN OFFICE

JUSTICE

POSTS

TRANSPORT

AGRICULTURE

ECONOMICS

LABOUR

HITLER
Fuehrer and
Chancellor

(All in existence in January 1933)

AVIATION   (Added 1933)

PROPAGANDA   (Added 1933)

SCIENCE AND EDUCATION   (Added 1934)

ECCLESIASTICAL AFFAIRS   (Added 1935)

At the beginning of the Nazi era, Reich government was divided among 10 ministries, and by 1935 the number had grown to 14. All ministry chiefs were cabinet members and their ranks were augmented by the granting of cabinet status to such Nazi leaders as Hess and Himmler. By these means, and also by the dismissal of DNVP leader Hugenberg, Hitler was able to increase the number of National Socialists in government from three to eight within a matter of months, although such numerical domination was insignificant alongside the creation of a Nazi-led Propaganda Ministry; under Goebbel's direction, this became one of the most vital props of National Socialist dominion. Because cabinet government had a short existence in the Nazi state, there was soon a serious vacuum of ministerial co-ordination and a certain trend towards ministerial and ministry polyocracy. Had Hitler consorted with ministers regularly and shown a broad interest in Reich administration and government, the problems would have been less. As it was, Hitler became increasingly remote from ministers and their offices, a number of whom grew quite skilled at exploiting the resulting silences and confusions.

Supreme Reich Authorities

The comparative independence of the various Reich ministries and their unco-ordinated actions were not, however, the sum of administrative chaos in the Nazi state. Yet greater problems stemmed from the practice of creating specialist government agencies which transgressed areas of ministerial jurisdiction but were never formally under them (Fig. 2.2). The first agency of this kind was the General Inspectorate of the German Road System, headed by Todt. The Reich Labour Service and the Office of the Four-Year-Plan were further examples. All these agencies were subservient only to Hitler. They were designated Supreme Reich Authorities and had powers to issue extraordinary decrees. They could operate without reference to each other or to the availability of resources. The administrative and organisational chaos created by these autonomous government agencies almost defies description, the more so because they seldom remained unchanged. And when coupled with the similar cleavages of jurisdiction among the Party *Reichsleiters*, some of whom also held Reich offices, the picture is even more confused. At some stage, it is logical to ask how far such a state of affairs was consciously created by Hitler or whether it grew through its own momentum. The answer probably lies somewhere between the two. Ill-defined, shifting and overlapping competencies were certainly an innate and inevitable feature of the operation of the *Führerprinzip*, especially given the way Hitler linked it with a considerable delegation of authority. However, there is no mistaking Hitler's 'divide and rule' tactics. Ever conscious of the potential for erosion of his ultimate control, he played off one institution against another – Party, Reich Ministries, Civil Service, Army – rarely failing to capitalise on the strengths and weaknesses of their various leaders. Needless to say, so complex did the internal structure of the Third Reich become, particularly from 1939, that it would have required a superhuman leader to be aware of its real nature and construction: to this extent, Hitler became a victim of his own creation; and it is here that the Nazi state displayed a volition of its own.

Whatever the degree to which the Supreme Reich authorities were alien to the traditions of administrative bureaucracy, it remains the case that some accumulated an impressive record of achievement in the shorter term. Fritz Todt, for example, was able to set up a state construction business which grew from being initially concerned with building the autobahn system to servicing the construction needs of the military and, later, the Nazi war machine at large. Because he had independent powers of legislation, Todt could conscript firms as well as workers, set prices and wages, and in general engineer an administrative apparatus which enabled his goals to be realised with maximum efficiency and speed. In this way, Hitler's Reich was capable of remarkable dynamism; the difficulty lay in sustaining such dynamism in the face of war and an entrenching polyocracy.

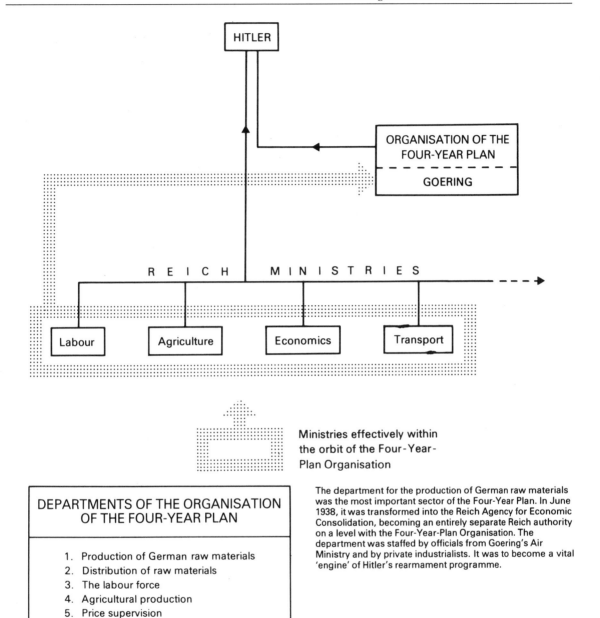

Fig. 2.2 The supremacy of the Four-Year-Plan Organisation in the traditional state bureacracy

The administration of territory

The chaos of authority and administration which characterised the central organs of state under Hitler invariably conveyed itself to the system of

Fig. 2.3 Economic regions (1943)

The administrative regions of the Economics Ministry with their regional offices circa 1943. The Gau Economic Chambers illustrate the creeping jurisdiction of the Nazi Party. They were established in 1942 to replace the 111 former Chambers of Industry. By this date, also, the Wehrkreise had taken on an increasing economic importance, notably in association with Speer's Armaments Ministry. Thus the power and jurisdiction of the Economics Ministry were becoming shadowy and ill-defined by the middle years of the war.

territorial organisation by which those organs were able to discharge their functions 'on the ground'. The Party had its territorial organisation in the Gaue; the Reich Ministries, the Supreme Reich Authorities, the civil service and the army all had theirs. Predictably, there was little spatial correlation

Fig. 2.4 Gau Thuringia, showing a few of the instances of low spatial correlation in administrative field systems. There was some coincidence of boundaries. Those for the Gau Thuringia were the same as those for the corresponding economic region (see map of economic regions). But neither of these matched the altogether larger territorial divisions of the Army (*Wehrkreise*) or of the Reich Labour Ministry (*Landesarbeitsamtsbezirken*). The Land Thuringia was actually smaller in area than the Gau, while the borders of the local administrative region for railways (*Reichsbahndirektion*) formed a pattern entirely their own.

among these various territorial organisations. Most had very distinctive systems of geographical division (Figs 2.3–2.5). Within the territories incorporated to form the Greater German Reich, moreover, the basic organisation often followed a different model altogether.

By 1938, the so-called 'field system' of the Finance Ministry split the Reich into 28 administrative divisions, whereas the Propaganda Ministry had 38. Likewise, the Ministry of Posts used a system of 46 subdivisions, while under the Transport Ministry there were 29 regions for railway administration. The Supreme Reich Authorities generated their own sets of field systems, as did the armed forces. Few of these systems matched, nor did they bear much relationship to, the Reich Ministry regions with which they were logically linked. The field system of the civil service was represented in what remained of the administrative organs of the federal state, namely the *Länder*, including Prussia and its separate provinces (Fig. 2.6). The civil service was under the Interior Ministry, but given the former sovereign rights of the *Länder* and the powerful tradition of the Prussian civil service organisation, it formed a power base of its own which its

HITLER
Fuehrer and Chancellor;
Party chairman

SUPREME REICH
AUTHORITY
X_1........

PARTY OFFICE
Hess, Deputy
Fuehrer

INTERIOR MINISTRY
- - - - - - - - - -
CIVIL SERVICE

ARMY
COMMAND

REICH MINISTRY
X_1........

——— Land/Province boundary
━━━ Gau boundary
- - - Wehrkreis boundary
—·— Ministry region boundary
—*— Supreme Reich Authority region boundary

Fig. 2.5 Schematic representation of conflicting territorial divisions circa 1936 (Atreich only)

Minister, Frick, sought to exploit in pursuit of his own designs on the Nazi dictatorship.

Aborted administrative reform

At several stages in the early history of the Nazi state, efforts were made to effect administrative reform. Territorial reform had been in the minds of many Gauleiters for some years; most of them sought to consolidate and enhance their geographical power bases. But the specific task of planning such a reform fell to Hess and his Office of the Deputy Führer. A draft

The following labels appear on the map:

Schleswig-Holstein, Mecklenburg, Pomerania, Danzig-West Prussia, East Prussia, District of Bialystok, Bre., H., Old, Hanover, P. of, B., Mark-Brandenburg, Wartheland, S.L., Br., Saxony, A., Westphalia, L., Nassau, Saxony, Lower Silesia, Rhine Province, Hesse, Hesse, Thuringia, Upper Silesia, General Government, Lu., Westmark, Sudetenland, Protectorate of Bohemia-Moravia, Lorraine, Württemberg, Bavaria, Lower Danube, O.V., Alsace, Baden, Ho, Upper Danube, Salzburg, Styria, Tirol-Vorarlberg, Carinthia, Upper Carniola, Lower Styria

The Länder, the Prussian provinces and the administrative areas of the Incorporated territories

0   200

km

Source: *Adm Hbk* II

Fig. 2.6 The Länder, the Prussian provinces and the administrative areas of the incorporated territories

The areas of civil administration in the expanded Third Reich circa 1942. They functioned as organs for the discharge of such services as health and education. Although many of the areas were direct descendants of the old sovereign states (free states under Weimar), they enjoyed little or no autonomy under Nazism. Power and decision-making rested fundamentally with the central Reich organisations.

document for the reconstruction of the Reich, submitted in February 1935, envisaged a system of *Reichsgaue* grouped in a series of economic-strategic circles around the German heartland, following closely the ideas of the geopolitician Haushofer. Reform of the machinery of central government became a major objective of Frick in conjunction with his Interior Ministry. In 1936 and again in 1937 he sought a regularisation of procedures and jurisdictions to combat the mounting chaos of ministerial and departmental polyocracy. However, neither of these reforms became a reality. There were too many conflicting views and Hitler constantly vacillated over their pursuance.

Administrative pluralism

A final distinguishing feature of Nazi government, which at times simplified but more often intensified its structural and jurisdictional chaos, was pluralism in the holding of offices (Fig. 2.7). This probably found most widespread expression in relation to the Party. The offices of Reich Governor (*Reichsstatthalter*) for the former *Länder* and their equivalent in the Prussian Provinces, the *Oberpräsidenten*, were largely filled by existing Gauleiters. Thus there was a fusion of personnel authority even if the territorial boundaries of the respective domains did not agree. The outcome was not necessarily harmonious, though. Because there were more Gaue in

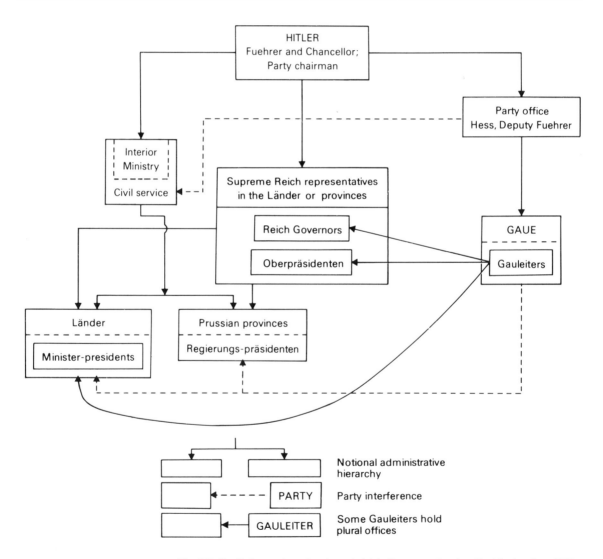

Fig. 2.7 Conflicting and overlapping administrative competencies: the Länder circa 1935

Prussia than there were Provinces, some Gauleiters failed to obtain posts of *Oberpräsident.* This encouraged friction in regional party-state relations and merely served to underline the depth of dualism which incongruent territorial systems forged. With the Reich Governors (*Reichsstatthalter*) as well as the *Oberpräsidenten*, there was an added problem over the precise nature of their authority. Whether they were subordinate to Hitler or to Frick, the Reich Minister of the Interior, was never properly clarified, for example. And their powers in relation to the various regional state officials – the *Regierungspräsidenten* in Prussia and the Minister-Presidents in the *Länder* – were likewise ambiguous.

Pluralism was also a characteristic of the Nazi elite. Indeed, the list of offices accumulated by leaders such as Goering was reminiscent of the pluralism of the medieval church. At various times, he ruled over the Reichstag and over Prussia, over the police and the Gestapo, and over aviation policy and rearmament. He was also Air Force Chief and in charge of the Organisation of the Four-Year-Plan. Goebbels enjoyed a power base of lesser breadth, but as Party Propaganda Chief, as head of the Propaganda Ministry and as Gauleiter of Berlin, he held a formidable springboard from which to influence German and Nazi alike. In this respect, Goebbels was a most effective exploiter of his pluralist holding, whereas Goering had far greater difficulty in reaping as efficient a return from his more disparate and unwieldy empire. The most successful Nazi leaders were undoubtedly those who held key Party and key Reich offices. In Hitler, of course, was to be found the apotheosis of the breed.

13 *Party organisation and administration*

The Nazi Party and its organisation represent a key to the understanding of the Third Reich. The Party's complex central apparatus, its regional and local constituents, the Hitler Youth, the SA and SS – all of these fulfilled roles and exercised influence which bore directly on the face of the Third Reich as it evolved over time and as it extended across Europe. It is important, though, to register that the Nazi Party remained separate from the Nazi state. There were elements of fusion, particularly of personnel, but beyond this, there were as many instances of dualism, sometimes reflecting basic differences of policy and action.

The Party itself was far from a model of consistency. The structure of its organisation was in an almost constant state of flux. And even where a seemingly stable organisational system can be identified, the operation of the *Führerprinzip* much restricted its real significance. Thus Gregor Strasser's wide-ranging reform of central Party organisation in 1932 (Fig. 2.8) provides only limited help in comprehending the sequence of policy decision and action. The newly created economic division IV, for instance, was quickly superseded by the NSDAP Reich Economic Council which Hitler established in September 1932, while the relative strengths of the various Party offices were largely a function of the closeness of their appointed leaders to the

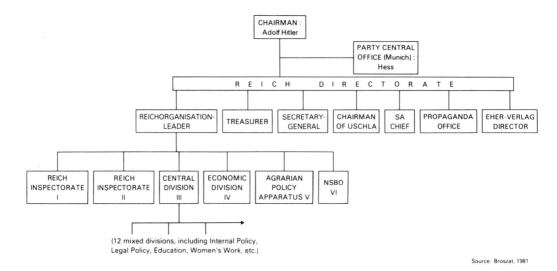

Source: Broszat, 1981

Fig. 2.8 Nazi Party central organization (1932–Strasser reform)

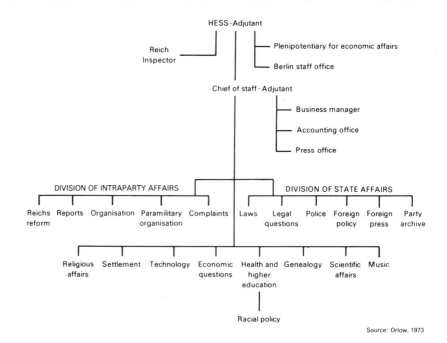

Source: Orlow, 1973

Fig. 2.9 Office of Deputy Führer (Late 1935)

person of the *Führer*. The pattern was one which prevailed right up to the collapse of the Third Reich in spring 1945.

The relative inconstancy of the Party organisation was yet more profoundly reinforced by the persistent rivalries between certain of its leading offices. Just as the importance of a particular office at any one time varied in accordance with the closeness of its leader to the *Führer*, so it also changed according to the success with which a leader was able to infiltrate the domains of others and so assemble a stronger power base. One of the most remarkable examples of this was found in the Office of Deputy Führer (Fig. 2.9), headed by Rudolf Hess until 1941 and then by Hess's former deputy, Martin Bormann. In the mid-1930s, the scale of this office grew phenomenally. By 1936, it had established a foothold in the operating spheres of most of the Party's *Reichsleiter*. At the same time, it began to try to exploit its position as supreme territorial authority in the Party, that is over and above the Gauleiters. From this potential power base, Hess and Bormann attempted to enhance the rule of Central Party Office at the expense of the other Party leaders (of policy areas or of territorial areas) who, predictably, resented and resisted such interference with their role as Hitler's derivative agents (Fig. 2.10 see pp. 64-5).

The Party as protector of the common people

The founding of the Nazi state presented some very real problems for the future of the Party; indeed, in certain respects, it signalled a watershed. In the decade to 1933, the Party machine became progressively geared to the task of acquiring power. It was seen in the way the Gaue coincided with the Reichstag electoral districts; it was apparent in the regional growth of the SA as a potential instrument of political coercion. But once the reins of power were in Nazi hands such functions lost much of their purpose. The SA presented the most serious problem in this respect; the murder of its leadership and its downgrading as a general organ of power were predictable events. For the Party machine, the task was one of redefinition of role and purpose. With the NSDAP established as the only political party, many of the standard functions of a political party became superfluous. Instead, the NSDAP became more and more a reservoir of ideology and an educator of the masses in the fundamental tenets of the Nazi political faith. The Party spawned a growing array of associate organisations designed to supplant ones already in existence: such bodies as the Nazi associations of women, of students, of youth, of teachers, of technicians and so on. In this way, German society became progressively honeycombed with Nazi ideas and practices. In its relations with the state, the Party increasingly assumed the role of ideological guardian and protector of the material interests of the masses. And the pattern became even more clearly crystallised in the case of the SS: the Party elite which became the specific guardian of Nazi racial ideology and which developed so that it almost formed a state within a state.

Party membership

At Hitler's accession, membership of the Nazi Party numbered around 850,000. By the middle of the war, this had risen to around 7 million (Fig. 2.11). Areas which before 1933 had shown only very limited acceptance of Nazism became some of the most buoyant in new recruitment, although industrial regions continued to lag behind agricultural ones in the degree of Party penetration. The dominance of the lower middle class remained a persistent feature of Party membership during the Third Reich's short

Fig. 2.10 The Nazi Party (by March 1945)

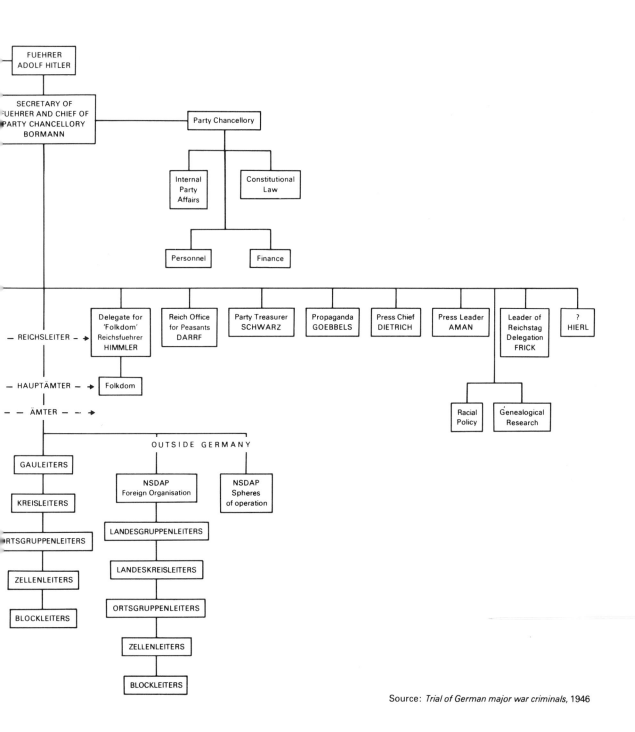

Source: *Trial of German major war criminals*, 1946

Fig. 2.11 Nazi Party membership

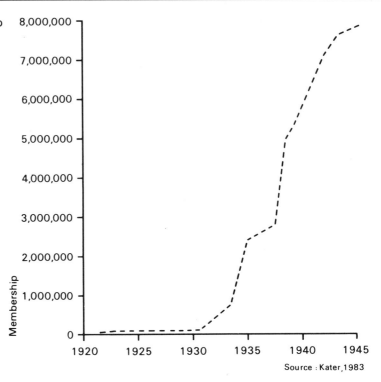

Source : Kater, 1983

Fig. 2.12 New party members, 1930–44

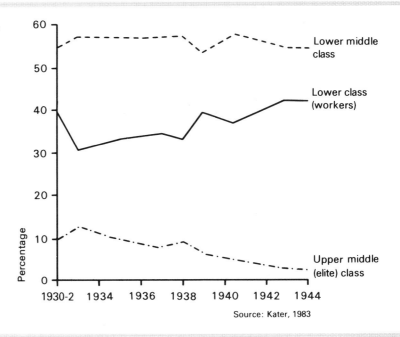

Source: Kater, 1983

existence, but from 1933 there was a secular upward trend in the proportion of the working class joining the Party (Fig. 2.12).

In January 1935, 65.5 per cent of the Party's membership were under the age of 41 and 37.6 per cent under 30, perpetuating the youthful character of

Fig. 2.13 Age distribution of party members: 1 Jan. 1935

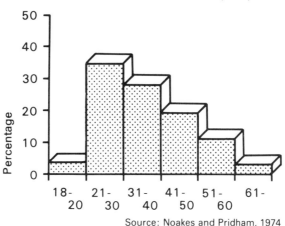

Numerical total of members : 2,493,890

Source: Noakes and Pridham, 1974

its earlier growth (Fig. 2.13). The pattern was facilitated by the SA purge of 1934, which removed many older Party stalwarts, and by the progressive elimination of the populist tradition in the Party led by Gregor Strasser before his removal in 1932.

In a country with a population of some 70 million by 1940, it may seem surprising that Party membership amounted to only about 10 per cent. In fact, this was part of a deliberate policy, dating back to 1933, to confine Party membership so as to form an elite. It would not be correct to infer from the relatively small scale of Party membership that this reflected the general status of Nazi influence in German society. Firstly, this would be to underestimate the Party's powers of intimidation and persuasion; secondly, it would gloss over the force represented by the many organisations affiliated to the Party: in this way, a majority of Germans became exposed or connected to the Party in some shape or form; lastly, it would neglect the influence on the masses exerted by Goebbels' new Propaganda Ministry, itself staffed largely by Party loyalists.

The Party's territorial organisation

One of the most important agencies of the strength of Nazi influence was found in its regional organisation. This was headed by the Gaue, a series of administrative regions which were adjusted and augmented as Hitler's goal of a Greater Germany was approached (Figs 2.14 and 2.15). By 1944, the Gaue were 42 in number and embraced the former Austrian state, the former Czech Sudetenland, parts of what was formerly western and northern Poland, and Alsace-Lorraine. The Gaue varied considerably in size and population; and those in the west were generally smaller than those in the east. The older Gaue closely resembled the Reichstag electoral districts, consistent with the Party's search for a Parliamentary road to power from 1924; they bore little relation to regular administrative divisions, either under Weimar or in the Third Reich. The new Gaue, however, made Party and civil administration as one. Thus Austria was divided into seven *Reichsgaue*, while parts of Poland

Fig. 2.14 The party regions: The Gaue (pre-1938)

1. Baden
2. Bavarian Ostmark
3. Düsseldorf
4. Essen
5. Franconia
6. Greater Berlin
7. Halle-Merseburg
8. Hesse-Nassau
9. Koblenz-Trier
10. Cologne-Aachen
11. Kurhessen
12. Kurmark
13. Magdeburg-Anhalt
14. Main-Franconia
15. Mecklenburg-Lübeck
16. Munich-Upper Bavaria
17. North Westphalia
18. East Hanover
19. East Prussia
20. Pomerania
21. Saarpfalz
22. Saxony
23. Schleswig-Holstein
24. Silesia
25. Swabia
26. South Hanover
27. South Westphalia
28. Thuringia
29. Weser-Ems
30. Württemberg-Hohenzollern

The party regions : the Gaue (pre-1938)

0   200

km

Source: Dickinson, 1938

annexed to make up Greater Germany were similarly treated, for example the *Reichsgaue* of Danzig-West Prussia and Wartheland. The office of Gauleiter was of special importance in the Third Reich. After such prominent Nazis as Goering, Himmler and Goebbels, the Gauleiters represented some of the most powerful Party officers; they were Hitler's direct representatives in the regions. Their influence was reinforced, moreover, by Hitler's practice of appointing some Gauleiters to offices of civil administration in the regions. Thus, although the boundaries of civil and Party administration were rarely coincident, the offices of their leadership sometimes were, even if the real power of those offices remained confused and subject to constant dispute.

The Gaue were at the head of four further subdivisions of the Party's regional and local administration: the *Kreise*, the *Ortsgruppen*, the *Zellen* and the *Blocke* – in descending order. In 1939, there were 822 Party *Kreise* (each with its own *Kreisleiter*), nearly 28,000 *Ortsgruppen* (covering sections of cities, small towns or country areas), nearly 93,000 *Zellen* (cells, consisting of assemblages of streets or other units), and some 480,000 *Blocke* (street blocks). Leadership and organisation in the local groups, cells and blocks were carried out largely by voluntary Party workers. But the Gauleiters and *Kreisleiters* had permanent offices and staffs. To a large degree, the Gau offices mimicked the functions and affiliations of Central Party Office.

Fig. 2.15 The Gaue (1944)

1. Baden
2. Bayreuth
3. Berlin
4. Danzig-West Prussia
5. Düsseldorf
6. Essen
7. Franconia
8. Halle-Merseburg
9. Hamburg
10. Hesse-Nassau
11. Karnten
12. Cologne-Aachen
13. Kurhessen
14. Magdeburg-Anhalt
15. Main-Franconia
16. Mark Brandenburg
17. Mecklenburg
18. Moselland
19. Munich-Upper Bavaria
20. Lower Danube
21. Lower Silesia
22. Upper Danube
23. Upper Silesia
24. East Hanover
25. East Prussia
26. Pomerania
27. Saxony
28. Salzburg
29. Schleswig-Holstein
30. Swabia
31. Steiermark
32. Sudetenland
33. South Hanover-Brunswick
34. Thuringia
35. Tirol-Vorarlberg
36. Wartheland
37. Weser-Ems
38. North Westphalia
39. South Westphalia
40. Westmark
41. Vienna
42. Württemberg-Hohenzollern

The Gaue (1944)

Source: *Adm Hbk* II

This map should be compared closely with that on the opposite page. Within the area of the Altreich, it shows how Gau-organisation remained largely unchanged, despite its increasing anachronism in the face of war and wartime exigencies.

14 *The army*

The armed forces and the German army in particular were comparatively unaffected by the Nazi takeover of power and remained so until early 1938. Historically, the army represented a formidable power block, resting on a long line of Prussian victories. The defeat of 1918 by no means destroyed its prestige and the highly coherent officer corps of the army remained intact. The provisions of Versailles, which restricted the army's size to 100,000 men were not insignificant, of course. But rearmament plans were being laid as early as 1928, five years before Hitler's accession, and from March 1935 conscription was reintroduced.

Opinions differ as to the part played by the army in the Nazi takeover. That Hitler enjoyed army support is undoubted. The question is over the forces which propelled the army to this position. The Nazis' plans for rearming Germany and their vigorous denials of Versailles were undoubtedly

Fig. 2.16 Military regions (1943)

The German Army had its own administrative areas (*Wehrkreise*) which served as bases for administration, recruitment and training of troops. Each area formed the home of an Army Corps, with the Corps Headquarters located in one of the major towns. The *Wehrkreis* boundaries were unrelated to any other administrative boundaries in the Third Reich, with the exception of the SS organisation after 1938.

attractive in many quarters of the officer corps. It is also clear that many army officers favoured a more authoritarian regime. Had the army wished to block the Nazi accession, it is clear that they would have succeeded, even in the face of the 400,000-strong SA. But army leaders were determined not to be drawn into a civil war. Thus Hitler's rise went unchallenged.

Between 1933 and 1939, the manpower of the German army expanded almost twentyfold. The number of active divisions rose from 10 to 51; by 1939, there were also 51 reserve divisions. For much of this expansionary phase, the army retained its traditional autonomy in relation to the German state. The technical head of the Army was the President, but under Hindenburg this amounted to nothing more than making the most senior appointments and observing ceremonial. Hitler did comparatively little to alter the position after his assumption of the presidency. In fact, he protected the army leadership from SS smear campaigns and allowed the army, generally, to stay aloof from the creeping supervision of the Party. Under the Reich Defence Law, no soldier was permitted to be a Party member. From early 1938, however, the pattern was altered radically. On 4 February, Hitler assumed direct command of all the armed forces and established the *Oberkommando der Wehrmacht* (OKW – Armed Forces High Command), which was effectively a military bureau for Hitler as Head of State and War Minister. The comparative independence of the armed forces was immediately reduced. And the army, although it represented over three-quarters of the armed forces, suddenly found itself placed on equal footing with the navy and the air force. Joint authority and responsibility under the War Ministry gave way to the Führer's will. The OKW became the tool of a warlord.

15 *The police state*

One of the peculiar features of the Third Reich was the degree to which it continued to use existing institutions. There was no wholesale revolution of the state administrative structure, for example, nor any thorough purge of its officialdom; and the army remained a largely autonomous organisation during the regime's first five years. In large measure, this pattern reflected the simple fact that the Nazis had no detailed plans for fundamental revolution. Indeed, the foundation and evolution of the Nazi state were characterised by a long succession of improvisations. Without a state monolith in the Stalinist mould, the Nazis relied for the maintenance of their authority on the spreading tentacles of party organisation and, above all, the police. The label 'police state' is a singularly appropriate one for the Third Reich. It was not only that the police were used to sustain the Nazi hold on power; they were also used to pursue the regime's special policies, including those on settlement and race.

The architect of the Nazi police state was Himmler, and its institutional bases the Gestapo and the SS. The Gestapo or *Geheimesstaatspolizei* (Secret State Police) was established by Goering in 1933 out of the old political police of Prussia. Goering was then Prussian Minister of the Interior. Subsequently the term Gestapo was applied to the political police of all the old *Länder* who by 1933–4 had come under the control of the SS and its leaders, Himmler and Heydrich. When Goering's Prussian Gestapo chief retired in spring 1934, Himmler succeeded him, bringing the entire political police organisation under SS tutelage. Seizure of control over the political police had been revolutionary rather than constitutional and the result was that the Gestapo became an organisation outside state jurisdiction, including the courts. This gave relatively free rein to totalitarian terror and the position was finally consolidated in June 1936 when Himmler was invested with the newly created office of Chief of German Police, which he exercised in conjunction with his office as *Reichsführer-SS*. The entire police force was subjected to centralised SS control and, although Himmler remained responsible to Frick, the Reich Minister of the Interior, this turned out in practice to be purely nominal. By 1943, Himmler was himself Reich Minister of the Interior, thereby ending the confusion altogether.

The physical size of the Gestapo was remarkably small: around 30,000 personnel in 1944. So one is left to wonder how it managed to inspire such widespread fear and terror among the civilian population. Was it primarily a function of the threat of arbitrary arrest and detention; of the interrogations and false confessions under the torture that might follow? Or was the answer more complex than this? One of the fundamental bases of Gestapo power was the climate of mutual suspicion that it generated within the mass populace. Almost every acquaintance and almost as many friends and relatives became potential informers or spies, even if the majority were not. But the efficiency of Gestapo power went beyond this. It rested also on the willingness of ordinary citizens to volunteer information – not necessarily because they supported Nazism *per se*, but because of bourgeois notions of the need to support prevailing authority, the more so if that authority appeared to be building upon attitudes which had a basis of popular support or consent, as seen for instance in anti-semitism.

The SS or *Schutzstaffeln* (guard detachments) originated in 1925 as Hitler's personal guard, but over the ensuing two decades developed into an inner elite of the Nazi Party, with the SS organisation itself forming what was almost a state within a state. Himmler was installed as leader of the SS in 1929 when the organisation numbered some 250 men. Thereafter, however, it expanded rapidly. By 1931, membership was around 10,000. This rose to some 50,000 in early 1933 and 200,000 in early 1935. There was a parallel development of SS organisations. In 1931, Himmler established an internal security service for the SS under Heydrich (the SD or *Sicherheitsdienst*). The aim was to protect SS ideology and to safeguard its leadership. The SS guards who had formed Hitler's bodyguard were expanded to form SS special duty troops (Fig. 2.17) and SS special guard groups for concentration camps. The former grew into the famous Waffen-SS (armed SS troops). The guard groups became the hated SS Death-head units. The SS was destined to become the new German elite, its members stringently screened so as to ensure racial and biological purity. Its officer corps was modelled by Himmler into a quasi-medieval order of knights complete with bizarre rituals. Within this corps, moreover, were many representatives from German aristocracy, echoing once again how the Nazi regime rested upon the co-operation and participation of the traditional German elites, even if the ultimate goal was to sweep them away.

The actual number of concentration camp detainees fluctuated wildly. For example, there were only about 3,000 prisoners at Buchenwald in May 1938, but by December of the same year this figure had risen to 17,000, only to fall again to 5,000–6,000 six months later. The total number detained at the time of the outbreak of war was just 25,000, only slightly less than the number in custody in mid-summer 1933. All this was a far cry from the

SS organisation 1937-8

— SS regions
• Site of divisions 1-80 of General SS

Source: Koehl, 1983

Fig. 2.17 SS organisation, 1937–8. From mid-1938, the SS regional organisation was adjusted to coincide with the army *Wehrkreise*.

714,000 detainees registered by January 1945.

The role of the concentration camp system (Fig. 2.18) in the early years of the Nazi state must necessarily be seen in conjunction with an increasingly repressive criminal law which gave rise to a rapid increase in regular imprisonment. There was a point in 1937, before Hitler's run of territorial annexations and the political repression that followed them, when the camps were actually beginning to appear redundant. Ultimately, though, the concentration camps became a linchpin of SS existence. And they provided penal colonies not only for political undesirables, but also for racial and social outcasts. They also formed sources of labour for SS enterprises (Fig. 2.19). By 1938, camp labour was being used for quarrying, road construction, market-gardening and handicrafts, not to mention the building

Fig. 2.18 Concentration camps, mid-1939

Fig. 2.19 SS enterprises (circa 1939)

of the concentration camps themselves. Thus was laid the framework for the SS slave empire which grew to yield an annual turnover in excess of 50 million Reichsmarks by 1943.

The size and power of the SS grew like a cancer as the short life of the Third Reich ran its course. The steady acquisition of police power was a primary stage. But by the middle of the war the Waffen-SS vied in authority with the army, the occupied territories were to all intents and purposes under SS domination, SS racist ideology was being put into practice in the mass killing of millions of Jews, and Himmler sat at the head of an economic empire which underpinned the diverse activities of his SS organisation, thereby contributing to the notion that the Third Reich was an SS state. By the last years of the war, the SS enjoyed an existence largely separate from the state administration and the Nazi Party. It had its own complex bureaucracy, some of which overshadowed the bureaucracy of the state and some of which reflected its role as ideological champion of National Socialism. It was in the nature of a special *Führer* executive, subordinate only to Hitler. But it also developed a leader-retinue structure of its own which contributed to the separatenes of its existence and the distinctiveness of its authority. Alongside the apparatus of the party, the state and the military, the SS formed yet another ingredient in the maze of incongruent jurisdictions which characterised the *Hitler state.*

One may well ask how a state which was so riven by internal rivalries and confusions could possibly develop the political and miltary power which enabled it to subjugate most of Europe. The question is much debated and cannot be easily resolved. Part of the answer lies in the fact that the bitter competition for power among the various ministries and agencies within the Third Reich tended to make these institutions individually more efficient, at least in the short term: thus the army became more ruthless as an occupying force in part in order to defend its position against the SS. The internal rivalries also helped to produce an explosive dynamism which was directed outwards: conquest provided the space in which the sectional appetites for power could be partly satisfied. But the Nazi political system never developed a plausible conception of a *status quo*, in which its various component parts were co-ordinated in a stable manner. It throve only on war, in which the parts were in continual motion, against each other as well as against real and imagined enemies.

III Part Three

Society

Nazi racialism

The racist doctrines of Hitler and his leaders were at the core of National Socialist ideology. They formed a vital propaganda tool in the seizure of power and in the consolidation of support among Nazi activists. They provided justifications for the regime's acts of aggression, notably in the east. And they offer insight into the self-destructive face of the Third Reich as its fortunes in war faded and popular assent became less secure.

As in so many of the Nazi regime's acts, it was the negative, destructive aspects of its racial doctrine which were pursued with most force. This was revealed most clearly in Nazi anti-semitism and found horrifying conclusion in the extermination camps of Himmler's SS. There was no clear consensus among National Socialists concerning the Jewish population, however (Fig. 3.1). Some Nazis saw the Jews in economic, not biological, terms, whereas

Fig. 3.1 Jews as a percentage of the German population, 1871–1933

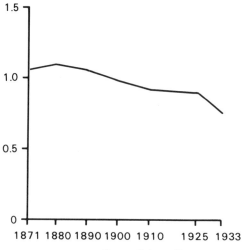

Source: Kwiet and Eschwege, 1984

Fig. 3.2 Jewish emigration from German territories, 1933-39

the biological anti-semitism of Hitler and Himmler, in which Jews were seen as parasites, was uncompromising and often manic in its force. It was from the latter view, of course, that the policy of physical extermination sprang. To this extent, the Holocaust was a Hitler, not a Nazi, creation.

The campaign against the Jews underwent a distinctive progression. It began with expulsion from defined professions: in April 1933, for instance, Jews were expelled from the civil service and universities. By September 1935, though, Hitler's own brand of anti-semitism had found formal expression with the Nuremberg Laws. These made marriage and sexual intercourse between Germans and Jews punishable by imprisonment. Three years later, in 1938, there began a mass expropriation of Jewish business concerns. And by November of that year, Nazi activists were engaged in mob violence against Jews and Jewish property. As the tide of anti-semitism grew, many Jews emigrated (Fig. 3.2). Some 320,000 had left by 1939.

For the Jews that remained, there was first a scheme for transporting them to Madagascar and later a plan to make East Poland or Siberia the reception area. However, this soon gave way to the so-called 'final solution:' the mass killing of not only Germany's Jews, but those of occupied Europe.

A much lesser-known facet of Nazi racial persecution were the policies aimed at homosexuals and other 'asocial' members of society, the Sinti and

Fig. 3.3 Part Jews (Mischlinge) were divided into two grades: those with two Jewish grandparents and those with one. Each category was subjected to varying degrees of discrimination.

Roma ('gypsies') principal among them. All were regarded as potential threats to the Nazi race project; the homosexuals because they made for a deficit in the sexual balance sheet. Most ended up in concentration camps. Many Sinti and Roma fell victim to mass killing: the 'final solution' to the 'gypsy question'.

A second plank of Nazi racial doctrine was the pursuit of racial purity (Fig. 3.3). This prompted laws encouraging marriage between healthy 'Aryan' Germans, granting financial bonuses for children of such marriages, and state assistance for illegitimates with 'Aryan' parenthood. A law for the protection of hereditary health became a basis of campaigns to sterilise the unfit and to liquidate, under the guise of 'mercy killing', the infirm, mentally defective and chronically diseased. Far less is known about the operation and effects of these eugenic plans than is of the campaign against the Jews. Owing to public disquiet, the regime was forced in 1941 to abandon the

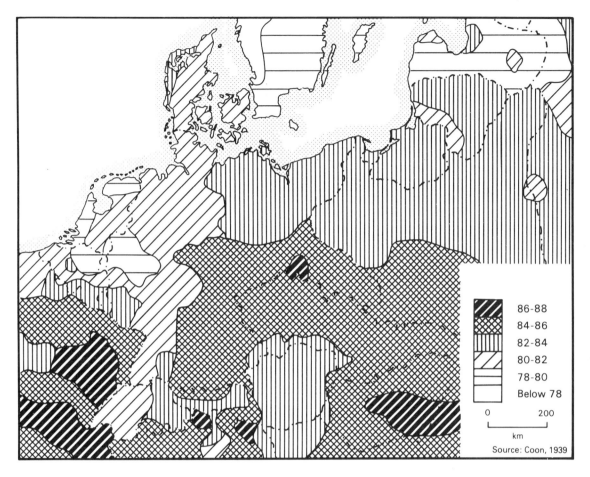

Fig. 3.4 Cephalic index. The cephalic index expresses the maximum breadth of the head as a percentage of its maximum length. As the map suggests, Nordic types demonstrated a low relative value, but there is clearly little basis to the idea that Germans as a whole matched this type.

mercy-killing scheme. Similarly, Himmler's own ideas for a Nordic polygamy, spearheaded in the SS, were never realised.

Underpinning these two primary facets of Nazi racialism were the dual beliefs of Nordic supremacy and Social Darwinism. The first asserted that the Aryan Nordic race, of which the German people incorporated representatives of varying purity, was the highest of all the races and the dynamic force behind modern civilisation. The second claimed that human history was the history of racial struggle, between higher and lower groups, with the Jews forming the basest and most dangerous of them.

The various doctrines making up Nazi racialism have long been discredited. The idea that Germany contained within it a biologically distinctive population is confounded by the evidence of physical anthropology. Germans of the Rhineland, for instance, show far greater affinities with their neighbours in the Low Countries than with their fellow

Prussians to the east. The idea, too, that there were to be found in Germany descendants of a pure race (in this case Nordic), is also unsupported by the evidence. Physical characteristics like the colour of hair and eyes are not inherited in groups but independently. The gene factors responsible for pigmentation, cephalic form (Fig. 3.4) and so forth are differently sorted in each generation. Hence the Nazis' picture of racial supremacy as presented in the tall, blonde, blue-eyed and narrow-headed German was a myth.

Equivalent objections can be made concerning the Nazi view that modern civilisation was spearheaded by Nordic or Aryan racial types. For example, the fundamental shift from hunting and gathering to settled agriculture from about the eighth millennium BC occurred first in the river basins east of the Mediterranean, the practice spreading to Northern Europe later. Similarly, there is little to the view that Nordic or Aryan types are superior in intelligence. In sum, one can state unequivocally that Nazi racialism had no scientific basis and was, to quote one early distinguished historian of the regime, 'a vast system of bestial, Nordic nonsense'. However, it is vital to appreciate that, whatever its untruths, Nazi racial dogma must be carefully examined if a proper understanding of the regime is to be formed. It represented a critical 'engine' of the *Hitler state*, one which changed progressively in pitch and power as the years passed. And the process was augmented and intensified by the way Nazi racialism was dressed up so that it *appeared* scientific. New university professorships were established in racial science, for example, and race studies became a subject for the state professional examinations. In schools, racial education became interlocked with the various pronouncements of the Nazi state in pursuit of racial purity, such that dicta learned in the classroom in one month could be observed being carried through in another. In propaganda terms, the 'science of race' had yet another dimension. The scientific label lent mystery as well as respectability in the popular mind. Thus legislation encouraging marriage between 'Aryan' Germans could be interpreted as essential social hygiene in the face of ill-understood or vague threats.

17 *Women*

Assessments of the role and status of women in Nazi Germany are not easily made. For instance, Nazi policies towards women were simultaneously paternalist and reactionary. And this position was not radically distinct from the policies and attitudes towards women that prevailed in Weimar Germany. In creating organisations devoted solely to the perceived role of women, the Nazis were both responding to political opponents who characterised the regime as anti-feminist as well as to the inexorable logic of totalitarian rule. But leadership within such organisations gave women an obvious sense of emancipation, not least because of the perks they enjoyed alongside male counterparts.

The central task of women within the Nazi state was undeniably that of procreation in pursuit of racial policy. At the time that in Britain, in December 1941, women were becoming part of a comprehensive and

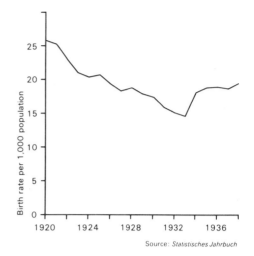

Fig. 3.5 (left) Number of marriages
Fig. 3.6 (right) Birth rate per 1,000 population

compulsory direction of labour, the number of German women in paid employment had been falling from 14.6 million in 1939 to 14.1 million in 1941. In 1933, in pursuance of a higher birth rate, the regime instituted a sequence of policies which has been viewed as among its most ingenious pieces of social engineering. From the summer of that year, marriage loans were made available for couples satisfying certain tests of economic, political and eugenic ability. For industrial workers, the loans represented four to five months' wages and the time-scale for repayment was a long one. More significant, the loan was reduced by a quarter upon the birth of each child. The immediate effect upon the marriage rate was dramatic (Fig. 3.5). In 1932 there were around 516,000 recorded marriages; two years later the figure had risen to 740,000. The rate was not sustained, however. The 1934 total was not exceeded until 1939, even if the aggregate picture for the 1930s was measurably greater than for the preceding decade. The effects on the birth rate were rather weaker (Fig. 3.6). By 1938, the annual rate had recovered to its pre-Depression level of around 19 per thousand, but it was still well short of the levels around 1920. It is certain that the eugenic tests associated with a marriage loan retarded the level of applications, even if the risk was in some cases more imagined than real. That average family size continued to show a decline has to be understood in terms of the latent forces of modernisation in which children were perceived as a burden, social as well as economic.

The marriage loan policy was complemented by various measures which were supportive of the maternal role: Mothers' Schools, improved maternity and welfare benefits, and better allowances. In parallel, attempts were made by the regime to limit contraceptive advice and availability, and abortionists were increasingly persecuted. These last measures were widely resented, not only in the eyes of women.

Emphasis on the maternal role had obvious merit in times of high unemployment. In fact, marriage loans were initially conditional upon the wife giving up work. The regime also blocked women's access to the labour market in other ways. They were prevented, for example, from working as judges or lawyers. And the campaign against women in public service, first instituted under Weimar in 1932, was steadily extended under Nazi rule. However, as Germany returned to full employment in the late 1930s, it made less and less economic sense to pursue measures of this sort; in wartime, it was positively counterproductive. But despite pressure from various power blocks within the Third Reich to achieve a full mobilisation of women, especially after the outbreak of war, the results were startlingly limited. In agriculture, the scale of women's participation grew, only this occurred largely by default. As more and more men were conscripted into the armed forces or left of their own volition for better paid jobs in factories, so the working of their holdings fell inevitably upon wives and mothers. The non- participation of many German women in the wartime labour force was compensated for by the drafting into the Reich of female workers from occupied territories. For them, as for many of the German women in agriculture, work was hard, conditions grim and the rewards minimal.

Ultimately, it seems, Nazi policy towards women has to be seen as inspired by political objectives. On the one hand, they were attempting to make an alternative to female emancipation; on the other, they were playing on the latent joys and stabilities of family life for men: soldiers and factory workers were more malleable when they knew their immediate kin were viewed as an object of care and reward by the state.

18   *Public welfare*

Germany under the Weimar regime pursued an enlightened and progressive welfare policy; and in Prussia the post-war period witnessed the establishment of a new Ministry of Public Welfare. One of the most notable features of Weimar legislation was the emphasis on the individual rights of the child, in particular that each German child should have the facility to be brought up physically, mentally and socially fit.

Under National Socialism, there were important changes in the goals of public welfare and in its underlying ideology. The individual became much less important than the community or body of the nation. Nazi racial dogma was then applied to this community with a view to 'breeding' a pure human stock in the Nordic/Aryan mould. Public welfare thus became racially discriminatory, especially with reference to Jews. And public welfare personnel were themselves subject to racial discrimination which resulted in a considerable loss of trained professionals, including some 5,500 Jewish doctors.

The Nazi Party had evolved an interest in public welfare long before January 1933. In the National Socialist state, this party machinery to some extent overlapped and duplicated that of the Reich Interior Ministry, which

Fig. 3.7 'Winterhilfe' expenditure, 1933/34 to 1940/41

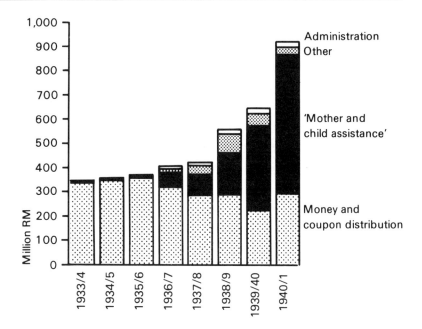

Source: *Wirtschaft und Statistik*, 1941

was responsible for public health, so that the familiar administrative cleavages of the *Hitler state* soon emerged to encourage inefficiency and waste. In terms of absolute numbers, there was a marked increase in registered doctors over the first 10 years of Nazi rule, aided by a two-year reduction in the length of training. But any expected benefits to the community at large were compromised by the medical demands of the Wehrmacht, the SS and various party organisations, together with the need to service a steadily extending land area. As a result, there was in some areas a dramatic decline in the ratio of practitioners per head of population, especially in the east. During the peacetime years alone, the ratio in the Reich as a whole is estimated to have fallen by 6 per cent.

The vigour of any distinctly National Socialist approach to public health was clearly circumscribed in some degree by the number and nature of trained professionals, but in less specialised branches of public welfare, involving financial and material benefits for groups like young mothers and children, or the very poor, the scope was considerably more open. From January 1933, in fact, all questions of charity and popular welfare were mandated to the National Socialist Public Welfare organisation or NSV (*Nationalsozialistische Volkswohlfahrt*). Even bodies like the German Red Cross became subordinated to it. The structure of the NSV echoed that of the Nazi Party itself, embracing a field system which extended down through the Gaue to Block level. At the same time, it developed a series of sub-groups or agencies, 'Mother and Child Relief' and 'Winterhilfe' perhaps the principal among them. *Winterhilfe* (Winter relief) was the most striking (Fig. 3.7). It formed a system of poor relief in which the NSV itself contributed only the propaganda. It relied on public charity, on door-to-door collections of money, food, bedding, clothing and other household items. In early years, the system was a logical, humane response to the plight of the unemployed millions. Once full employment had been achieved, the needs were ostensibly less evident or immediate, yet the system continued to be expanded, especially during the war. In fact, *Winterhilfe* ultimately became a massive 'gratuitous ritual', aimed at raising popular feeling and inculcating self-sacrifice. It operated from October to March, was elaborately and ingeniously thought out, was invariably inaugurated in a wave of publicity, and, for the dedicated Nazis, became a test of political faith for the masses. Failure to give to *Winterhilfe* at all was strongly condemned, as was failure to give enough. Thus what was made out to be a voluntary charity was effectively a compulsory tax which ate into workers' wages, making some of them in turn liable to be recipients of relief. The system became self-fulfilling. In 1937/8, for instance, at a time when the unemployment problem had largely been solved, some 8.9 million received relief. Following Nazi racial goals, *Winterhilfe* was distributed only to those satisfying the appropriate racial and biological criteria. More sinister was the involvement of the NSV at large in racial selection. Its kindergarten in occupied territories became staging posts for the Germanisation of those children satisfying Nazi racial criteria. The unfortunates who failed the test were taken to special homes for young children where they were deliberately starved to death.

19   *Education*

The ultimate goal of Nazi education policy was the creation of 'the political, National Socialist human being'. Education was not to be training towards free, independent activity, but was to develop the abilities of young Germans so that they fulfilled the aims and desires of the Nazi state. The reorganisation of the education system on Nazi lines had a number of distinctive dimensions. It involved an extensive revision of the curriculum. It involved the progressive removal of political and racial undesirables from the profession of teachers. It embraced the establishment of a stream of specialist schools where the future Nazi elite was to be trained. Finally, it applied the *Führerprinzip* to the whole structure of educational administration and brought the professional teaching organisations firmly within the Nazi orbit. Certain of these aims were more quickly achieved than others: the purge of teachers, as well as the co-ordination of administration in accordance with the *Führerprinzip*. By the close of 1933, for instance, most Jewish teachers had been dismissed. The nazification of the curriculum was more protracted and initially fell prey to some of the rivalries of the *Hitler state*, notably between the Education Ministry and Hess's Central Party Office. Curriculum consolidation was hampered, anyway, by a declining supply of teachers and money, a feature which grew more serious after the outbreak of war. The enormous stress that the Nazis laid on physical education also slowed the learning process, regardless of the burdens that may have been imposed by a novel ideology. Pupils could

Fig. 3.8 German universities

spend up to five hours a day engaged in sports. There was also a latent conflict with the Hitler Youth, which set a rival focus for children's energies and loyalties. After 1933, pupils of non-Aryan origin attended German schools only by privilege. Where they did so, many were subjected to discrimination and ridicule. Jewish communities sought to expand the number of specifically Jewish schools, but such responses were to become irrelevancies in the face of policies of liquidation: by June 1942, for instance, Jewish children were prohibited from school attendance altogether.

Under National Socialism, the German universities saw a substantial decline in the numbers of both students and teachers (Figs 3.8 and 3.9), as well as a steady diminution in the range and quality of scholarship. In 1930, the number of matriculated students at the summer semester had reached a post-war peak of almost 130,000; by the outbreak of the Second World War, it was less than half this level. The nazification of curricula and the

Fig. 3.9 Technical colleges and
colleges of economics and
political science

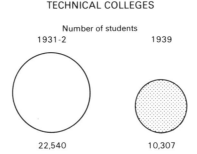

TECHNICAL COLLEGES

Number of students

1931-2   1939

22,540   10,307

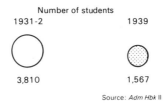

COLLEGES OF ECONOMICS AND POLITICAL SCIENCE

Number of students

1931-2   1939

3,810   1,567

Source: *Adm Hbk* II

concomitant restrictions upon academic freedom made university life
increasingly unattractive. Non-Aryans were excluded from university; and
those who could not show a satisfactory record in the Hitler Youth were also
ineligible. Other explanations were found in the increasing career
opportunities in business and in the armed forces (especially for men) as the
Third Reich moved to a war footing. Earlier, in 1933, the number of
students had actually been cut by law, on account of very high graduate
unemployment. During the great phase of Nazi *Gleichschaltung* (1933–4),
the universities lost some 16 per cent of their staff in a wave of ejections.
The technical institutes lost around 10 per cent, the law schools some 21 per
cent. Many of the more distinguished scholars took to emigration.

National Socialist schools

The establishment of specialist or elite schools in the Third Reich displayed
most of the familiar conflicts which characterised the regime (Fig. 3.10).
The *Napolas*, for instance, were the creation of the Education Ministry and,
from the date of their inception (1933), grew to number 35 later in the war.
In the meantime, in 1937, the Hitler Youth leader and the head of the
German Labour Front had established the Adolf Hitler Schools, run and
financed largely by the Party. Perversely, though, Hitler appeared to favour
the *Napolas* and subsequently set about encouraging their wider extension,
helped by personnel from the SA and the SS. Even so, there was no clear or
consistent curriculum in either school. Above all, they were institutions
which looked to train bodies not minds. And much the same could be said
of the *Ordensburgen*, established by the head of the Labour Front as a kind
of alternative to higher education and as the final forcing ground for the next

NAPOLAS
(National Political Educational Institutes)

Ages : 10-18; established 1933 onwards, partly modelled on old Prussian cadet schools. Formally under Education Ministry, but senior personnel from SA and SS. There were 23 Napolas by 1940, containing almost 5,000 pupils, nearly all of them male. Majority of graduates entered armed forces.

AHS
(Adolf Hitler Schools)

Ages : 12-18; established 1937 onwards; operated and financed exclusively by the Nazi Party. Intended as training schools for future Nazi leaders. Selected graduates eventually enter the ORDENSBURGEN. Of the first group of graduates (1942), 67 per cent chose political leadership for their careers.

ORDENSBURGEN
(Order Castles)

Curriculum

1. Racial, biological and ideological education

2. Sport and physical training

3. Political education

LANGEMARCK SCHOOLS

Designed to aid pupils of poor parents to gain the necessary qualifications for university entry. Selection made in mid-teens. Successful entrants underwent eighteen months' training.

Fig. 3.10 National Socialist Schools: Secondary Schools

generation of Nazi leaders. Entrants spent five years circulating among the remarkable fortress sites. No such training was adequate for the SS, though. Himmler's organisation had its own educational designs and was deeply suspicious of alternative forms of educational reproduction.

Nazification of the curriculum

Curriculum development in the service of National Socialism presented a formidable task for Party and state officials. That progress was haphazard and the actual results often dubious is a reflection of this, especially given the regime's relatively short life-span. The censorship of school textbooks was one of the first and perhaps most readily implemented strategies, and yet this was not directed centrally until the spring of 1938; up to that time teachers performed the task of censoring. The institution of guidelines for elementary and secondary school curricula was similarly slow, even given that the task was no simple one. The brakes on more rapid progress were the desires of the various power groups within the Third Reich to influence education for their own ends. Subjects such as history and geography were variously recast to reflect Nazi racial doctrines. *German* history was studied largely to the exclusion of all other, and focused on Hitler and the rise of National Socialism. Vain attempts were made to interpret the Third Reich as the apotheosis of specified developments and trends in German history. German literature was sifted and categorised so that blood ties and sense of community were thrown into greater relief, and explicitly *völkisch* literature was emphasised as part of this. Religious instruction was increasingly replaced by a motley collection of anti-Christian nationalist ideas, the change enhanced by the steady abolition of confessional schools. In the natural sciences, biology (predictably) was revised in accordance with Nazi racial theories, and racial science was granted an academic status which justified the establishment of new professorships in the universities. Many of the more mature among the German people held undeniable misgivings about the distortion of historical perspectives and the ascientific nature of some of the regime's teachings. In German youth, however, Nazism found an understandably more receptive constituency, one which was cultivated as much outside the schoolroom as in it. The ideological campaign in the schoolroom was complemented in the machinery of the Hitler Youth.

20   *The Hitler Youth*

By early 1939 the Hitler Youth had a little over 7.25 million members, age 10 to 18, including girls (Fig. 3.11). From December 1936, all German young people were required to be educated in the Hitler Youth, physically, intellectually and morally. But even before that, it counted a significant proportion of German youth among its members through absorption of existing youth organisations and dissolution of others. The Roman Catholic groups were the most resistant. They were eventually brought into line by the Gestapo which occupied and closed the group's headquarters in Düsseldorf, arresting many of its leaders.

The title *Hitler Youth* is of particular significance. Although the movement started life under SA control and hence within party jurisdiction, by late 1936 it had the status of a Supreme Reich Authority, largely outside

Fig. 3.11 The expansion of the Hitler Youth

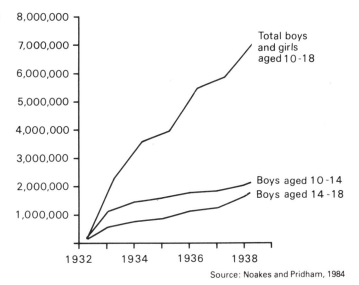

Total boys and girls aged 10-18

Boys aged 10-14
Boys aged 14-18

Source: Noakes and Pridham, 1984

The training scheme set out for use in the Hitler Youth's 'toughening-up' camps for war services, 1944

1. The war
2. The enemies of Germany
3. Our Volk
4. The Fuehrer and the movement
5. The fundamentals of our ideology
6. Volk and race
7. Our socialism
8. The Reich

Source: *Glauben und Kämpfen* (Berlin, 1944)

The section 'the enemies of Germany' included the following examination of Jews:

1. Is this also a German?
2. The Jew, creator of the Marxist heresy
3. Every German is an anti-semite
4. The Jew is condemned to destroy humanity
5. The unheroic fundaments of Jewry
6. What does the Jew, Rawage, say?
7. Is there a Jewish riddle of the universe?
8. They stand the law of nature on its head
9. The Jew is uncreative
10. Our war against the Jewish parasites

party and ministry jurisdiction, headed by Baldur von Schirach who was answerable solely to Hitler. In other words, the Hitler Youth represented a further outflanking of orderly command structures within the Third Reich.

The public face of the Hitler Youth was one which emphasised *community* and *partnership* in the service of the entire German people. Nazi propaganda techniques subsequently channelled this community awareness towards a specific destiny: the birth of a new German empire. And as the prospects for this empire grew, the Hitler Youth was increasingly drawn into its realisation. Training sessions became more and more militaristic in character. In effect, the Hitler Youth became an armed force in the making, a seed-bed for militarist aggression. Thus resulted the ultimate paradox: a movement which enshrined the partnership of youth and encouraged self-reliance and co-operation became increasingly co-ordinated in the service of a regime seeking to divide society under ruthless authoritarianism.

The appeal of the Hitler Youth to German adolescents was that it provided opportunities for individual self-assertion: the organisation was run largely by members themselves, even if this led to much indiscipline and denunciation. Some elements of German youth, though, never succumbed to its attractions. In part this can be understood in the time-honoured tradition of youth rebellion which characterises the culture of western materialism. But it was also due to political and ideological objections. All such opposition was dealt with through the familiar Nazi institutions of terror. A rather different brake upon the totalising designs of the Hitler Youth was found in the competition it met from the Reich Ministry of Education. The Minister, Bernhard Rust, succeeded in limiting the direct influence of the Hitler Youth in Schools, even if the discipline of the movement, with its glorification of the physical over the intellectual, could not fail to colour the atmosphere in the classroom.

21   *Culture*

Under National Socialism, cultural life in any true sense disappeared. All aesthetic means were appropriated towards political ends. In effect, the aesthetic became a vehicle for the legitimisation of National Socialism. The pattern was most forcibly represented in radio broadcasting and on public newsreels, but no part of the cultural product escaped corporate control under the ever-present eye of Goebbels as Minister for Popular Enlightenment and Propaganda.

The Reich Chamber of Culture, established in November 1933, provided the central agency through which the aesthetic in Nazi Germany was controlled and co-ordinated. The Chamber covered art, literature, music, theatre, the Press and broadcasting. Former professional associations were transformed into corporate professional groups, membership becoming compulsory for anyone wishing to practice their particular skill. In parallel, the *Führerprinzip* was established as the central organising principle. Goebbels and his various subordinates were thus able to intervene at will, a feature that took on added significance given the nihilism of most policy-making within the Chamber and its various sub-groups.

The most populist facet of National Socialist culture was its anti-modernist stance, particularly in the visual arts and in architecture. All modern art, for example, was rejected as degenerate, whether or not it was abstract. The reason why this nihilist attitude struck chords with the masses was the way it echoed disillusionment with modern industrialism, with the crises of capital, especially during the 1920s. Beyond the rejection of the modern, though, the Nazis cultivated a pattern which reflected and supported their ideology, satisfied the cultural pretensions and social separateness of their elites, and countered or masked deteriorating fortunes in war. Thus the works of Jews were summarily banned. Farmer, factory worker and soldier were cast as idyllic partners of social production. Allegorical themes saw a resurgence. And historic wars and conflicts were resurrected and mythologised.

Among the most pervasive themes of National Socialist culture was the

Fig. 3.12 above Franz Eichhorst
Mutter und Kind

Fig. 3.14 above right Carl Baüm
Pflüger am Oberrhein

Fig. 3.15 below right   Franz
Eichhorst *Maschinen Gewehrnest*

'heroic'. It was seen, for instance, in Hitler's passion for Wagnerian opera. It found most lasting and perhaps most vivid expression in the monumental architecture of the Third Reich. The massive granite and marble-faced edifices created by Hitler and his architect, Albert Speer, were intended as 'Parthenons' of later millennia. Monopoly capital benefited enormously from the building boom that such architectural projects engendered. Moreover, profits were enhanced by the use of concentration camp labour in stone-working. Even for regular labour, though, the material rewards were correspondingly weak. In the eyes of the political elite, the skill and muscle power invested in such projects was seen as enough reward in itself.

The aesthetic in Nazi Germany held an especially prominent position in mass political discourse. In what has been styled as the 'aestheticisation of politics', the vacuity of the Nazis' political project at large was compensated for by the mass rallies and rituals, by the carnival and the festival. The psychic experience of the annual Nuremberg rally is hard to underestimate, but its impact was temporary and so ceremonialism was extended to embrace existing elements of popular culture, Christmas perhaps offering one of the more striking (and ironic) of these.

It has been suggested by some commentators that, although National Socialist cultural policy was not without some measure of popular consent, it nevertheless precipitated a retreat into 'non-political privacy'. It remains true, however, that there was little escape from the anti-Jewish posters in tramcars and on bill-boards, from the slogans which proclaimed faith in the Führer, or from the swastikas that hung or flapped from every public building. In the home, moreover, the radio provided a liturgy all of its own: in the Führer's speeches, for example, or in the seemingly interminable announcements which recounted the progress of the war, all prefaced by hysterical trumpet fanfares. As the Nazi Empire faded from 1942, ordinary people had increasing difficulty reconciling the claims of the official broadcasts with what they learnt from other sources. But this tended to diminish rather than destroy the *Führer* myth. There are those households who can still recall the hush which descended upon Hitler's last New Year broadcast in 1945.

22 *Religion*

The geography of religion in Nazi Germany (Fig. 3.15) was distinctive in several ways. Protestants dominated in northern and central Germany (Fig. 3.16), but to the west and south there was a progressive preponderance of Roman Catholics, some 70 per cent in Bavaria. In 1933 the ratio of Protestants to Roman Catholics was roughly two to one. With the reincorporation of the Catholic Saar territory in 1935 and, later, the annexation of Austria and the Sudetenland, both Catholic, that figure altered to almost one to one – Protestants retaining a very slight majority.

German Protestantism had long been a political force. Prussian hegemony in Germany after 1871 drew extensive support from the conservative/ Protestant stratum and Lutheranism became a pro-state creed. The Nazis enjoyed much the same basis of support, as the geographical pattern of the

Fig. 3.15 Religions in Germany

Protestants

Roman Catholics

Mixed

Other

1919 frontiers

0   200
km

Source: *Adm Hbk* II

Berlin

Warsaw

Vienna

Fig. 3.16 Länder/provinces more than 70 per cent Protestant

0   200
km

Länder/provinces more than 70 per cent Protestant

July 1932 Reichstag elections bears witness. Roman Catholicism formed a long-standing rival to Prussian authority, not least within the borders of Germany itself. And the determined reluctance of Roman Catholics to support National Socialism before 1933 clearly illustrates this. In fact, Roman Catholicism in Germany was yet more politically identified in that it had its own party political base: the Centre (Zentrum). But, somewhat paradoxically, it was this unity, coupled with the authoritarian structure of the Roman Catholic Church, which saw Catholic opposition largely localised upon the conclusion of the Reich Concordat with Rome on 20 June 1933. The contrast was with the Protestant Church, which, under the co-ordinating pressures of Nazism, began to display its diverse origins and structure. There had never been a united Protestant Church in Germany. The Nazis initially sought one under their own political banner, but failed decisively.

As the Third Reich ran its course, the relationship between National Socialism and the churches proved increasingly ambiguous. Many Nazi leaders were atheists and wished to erode the influence of Christianity, but most of their supporters thought of themselves as Christians. The ecclesiastical realm was subjected to a campaign of co-ordination (*Gleichschaltung*) in the way of every other sector of society under Nazism. Included in this was the exclusion of 'racial undesirables' from the clergy. At a very early stage the Nazis succeeded in depoliticising the Catholic Church with its prominent party political representation. Moreover, the clergy, like so many other professional groups, also fell increasingly prey to the persecution and terror of the SA, the Gestapo and the SS organisations. Against this backcloth, though, there emerged the so-called 'church struggle', involving Catholic as well as Protestant churches, and embracing passive opposition from the pulpit on the one hand, and vigorous campaigns like the one to retain the crucifix in schools on the other. The Nazi response to such resistance was typically a cautious one. Some party activists sought a renewed programme of co-ordination and persecution. But Hitler was especially sensitive on religious issues and attempts to extend control over the churches were characterised by persistent reversals, often at Hitler's will. A separate Reich Ministry of Ecclesiastical Affairs was established in 1935, but even by the middle years of the war and notwithstanding the atheism of most sections of the Nazi leadership, the relationship of the churches to National Socialism remained unresolved. The Church Minister, Kerrl, took the view that National Socialism needed Christianity because it had nothing with which to replace it. Thus religious faith became a passive support, almost an unwelcome surrogate for faith in National Socialism, impossible to attack frontally during the war. The various festivals of the Nazi calendar, even if they were designed as much to be cultural as political events, had little impact on religious observance.

23   *Farm entailment*

Among the various sectors of German economic production, agriculture was one of the most rapidly co-ordinated in the service of National Socialism. In part this was due to Nazi penetration of many agrarian organisations prior to 1933. It reflected, too, the relative strength of Nazi support in the agricultural sector, which was reinforced by substantial measures of economic relief for farmers in 1933. But it was also linked to the ideological significance attached to agriculture in the goals of National Socialism. Hitler, in his alliance with his agrarian policy chief, Darré, saw the agricultural peasantry as the core of future German nationhood and a prime vehicle in the consolidation of the Greater German Reich. The communion of blood and soil (*Blut und Boden* or '*Blubo*') became a pervasive image, to be echoed in art and in literature. The outcome was that among the policy measures of National Socialist agriculture were laws on the entailment of peasant holdings. These were deliberately aimed to preserve the bonds of blood and soil in perpetuity. Agricultural holdings of between 7.5 and 125 hectares were tied to active farmers of German blood and to their direct descendants in perpetuity. The entailed farms became known as *Erbhöfe* (Fig. 3.17) and the proprietor-farmers were designated *Bauer*. The latter term was subsequently used exclusively with reference to entailed farms. Local *Erbhof* courts became the exclusive organs of entailment. In regions where partible

Fig. 3.17 Entailed farms (*Erbhöfe*): 1939

**Entailed farms
(*Erbhöfe*): 1939**

Area of *Erbhöfe* as percentage of all farmland and afforested land

- 50-65
- 40-50
- 30-40
- 20-30
- 10-20
- 5-10

(excludes holdings below 0.5 ha)
Source: Hilgeman,, 1984

0   200

km

inheritance systems prevailed, the practice had been for farmholdings to be granted to the eldest male heirs and for remaining children to be given money payments. Under the entailment laws, such payments were restricted to farmholdings' current receipts in an attempt to curb indebtedness. In Prussia, entailment was established in May 1933. The Reich Entailment Law followed in September 1933.

The *Erbhöfe* never covered more than about one-third of all farms, and they contributed little to the improvement of agricultural efficiency. The farming community itself was not enamoured with entailment. Many viewed the legislation as restrictive on freedom and on the new guarantees against sequestration in cases of farm indebtedness, even with the compensations of guaranteed prices which were introduced almost simultaneously under the newly formed Reich Food Estate. Outside the entailment legislation were the mass of small-holdings, as obvious an arena for land reform as any, and then at the further extreme the vast Junker estates east of the Elbe. In 1938, 2.5 million of the smallest farmholdings had less land area than the top 1 per cent of holdings (Fig. 3.18). Had entailment been part of a comprehensive land reform programme, some improvement in efficiency might have been obtained. Such a reform had certainly long been in the party programme. But as became so typical of National Socialism in practice, party commitments were implemented haphazardly, the more immediate needs of the regime readily holding precedence. Radical land reform would have compromised the regime's drive for agricultural self-sufficiency in preparation for war. Entailment, therefore, was hardly a political measure and even less an economic one. Most of all it was part of the great myth propagated by the Nazis about the rebirth of German nationhood – the anticipated *völkisch* empire. The regime organised its own annual harvest festival, supposedly

Fig. 3.18 Entailed holdings by size

symbolic not only of the fruits of the soil but of the union of the sexes. *Erb Bauer* were encouraged to resurrect the wearing of folk costume. In turn, they and their families stared down from paintings by favoured Nazi artists, actors in a pastoral idyll.

24   *The Labour Front*

The working classes were never fertile ground for the National Socialists. Attempts to win their support in the late 1920s through a Nazi Party factory cell organisation, the Nationalsozialistische Betriebszellenorganization (NSBO), made little headway. And by the time Hitler held the reins of power, the working-class organisations, notably the trade unions, remained as an independent power block, considered by some to have been among the best organised labour movements in the industrial world. However, in a classic *coup d'état*, the Nazis smashed trade union power on 2 May 1933, having only a day previously courted union goodwill by declaring 1 May (International Labour Day) a national holiday. In place of the unions, the Nazis established the German Labour Front (*Deutsche Arbeitsfront* or DAF), led by Robert Ley. The DAF was a highly improvised and ill-defined organisation, qualities which were to bring forth a long succession of disputes and rivalries within the polycratic structure represented by the Third Reich. The DAF was not a state organ but an auxiliary arm of the Nazi Party. However, its links with the Party were close enough, given that Ley was staff leader of the Party's political organisation at the same time as being DAF leader. The DAF in fact mimicked in general terms the organisational structure of the Party with its large central office and with its 13 territorial divisions, the latter divided into Kreise and these split into local groups. But this neighbourhood organisation was ultimately over-shadowed, in practical terms, by the factory-centred organisation, or *Betriebs-gemeinschaften*. Factory managers (*Betriebsführer*) were required to follow standards set by the DAF and to seek model status for their firms.

The overwhelming paradox of the German Labour Front was that although it ultimately had some 25 million compulsory members and received vast sums in membership dues, it never represented them in any material sense. Despite repeated efforts by Ley, the DAF never won power to negotiate wages, for example. This rested with the Trustees of Labour (*Treuhänder der Arbeit*), state officials whom Hitler appointed in mid-June 1933. It was this absence of wage-bargaining power that persuaded employers to adopt a positive attitude when moves were made for their incorporation into the DAF later in 1933.

The underlying ethos of the DAF was one which sought to create a 'people's community' in place of the class conflict of capitalist industrial society. The factory was to become a partnership which would raise productivity and generate pride in the collective achievement, echoing in certain measure the Fordist production regime in the United States. Bereft of any direct power over worker conditions, the DAF launched a compaign

Fig. 3.19 Organisation diagram for *Strength through Joy*, from Der nationalsozialistische Schulungsbrief, 1934

(Fig. 3.19) under the label 'Strength through Joy' (*Kraft durch Freude*). This sought to compensate for the strains of industrial labour by sponsoring cheap holidays and entertainments on a national scale. At the same time, a Department of the 'Beauty of Work' (*Schönheit der Arbeit*) was created within the DAF, the object being to enhance the aesthetic appearance of the workplace. The ultimate measure, however, was the programme for a 'People's Car', the *Volkswagen*. In outward appearance, the DAF was clearly taking on the mould of a propaganda organisation but in an indirect way it was also gaining an economic power base. Its holiday schemes, for instance, became crucial to the prosperity of the German holiday industry at large and provided enormous revenues for the railways. The initiation of the Volkswagen programme signalled a foothold in the motor-vehicle industry. The DAF sought more direct increments to its power with its entry into vocational training in 1936–7 and, increasingly, Ley proceeded to capitalise on his dual positions as a party Reichsleiter and as leader of the DAF. The power echelons of the Party were exploited by the Front's massive organisational apparatus such that its regional leaders to some extent vied in authority with the Party's Gauleiters and Kreisleiters. In fact, the DAF grew to become the largest organisation in the Third Reich, readily eclipsing the Nazi Party, in funds as well as in membership. Its bureaucracy alone ran to 40,000 individuals.

In the final years of peace, it was the singular pursuit of power rather than the condition of labour which guided the German Labour Front's activities. And this was against a background of growing labour crisis, notably a shortage of skilled labour, from 1936 onwards. Whatever propaganda means were devised to wed the working classes more firmly to the goals of National Socialism, circumstances conspired to make the power of labour largely independent of them. As shortages of labour in the booming metal, engineering and construction trades became more acute, wage spirals and the pirating of workers by employers became widespread. It was perhaps not surprising, then, that traditional working-class consciousness remained relatively intact, despite the terror of the Gestapo and the SS in industrial districts like the Rhine-Ruhr. Worker opposition became manifest not in organised protest but in suspicion, in individual acts of non-co-operation, and in refusals to accept the Labour Front's propaganda. In the prelude to war, the regime made movements towards a comprehensive direction of the labour market, but the measures were piecemeal and often indecisive, and the population slow to conform. The Labour Front actually got in the way of such efforts and continued to make populist propaganda. It was the inmates of the concentration and work camps who were to become the real labouring class of National Socialism: at once impressed, servile and unremunerated, where '*Kraft durch Freude*' was anathema.

25 *Law and justice*

From the very outset, National Socialism perverted the legal system in its own service. The prosecution of the Reichstag 'arsonists' in 1933 on the basis of a law passed after the event transgressed a fundamental legal principle. Special courts (*Sondergerichte*) were established following the Reichstag Fire Decree to try those committing offences under its provisions. They were political courts as such, and the judicial procedures were streamlined in ways which contravened primary legal conventions. The number of *Sondergerichte* grew from 13 in 1933 to over 70 by 1945. The People's Court (*Volksgericht*) in Berlin, also established in 1933, functioned to try acts of treason (Fig. 3.20).

The German judiciary was only slowly subjected to large-scale Nazi interference. Its relationship with National Socialism was much the same as that of the civil service and the army; all were institutions which had to be maintained for the efficient working of the state machine, Nazi or otherwise. The judiciary engaged in tacit co-operation with the regime, many seeing political interference in terms of longer-term national good. Some jurists also looked towards the creation of a distinctly National Socialist body of law in

Fig. 3.20 The distribution and
growth of political courts, (a) circa
1934, (b) 1943

The distribution and
growth of political courts
Circa 1934

0   200
km

1943

The People's Court
▲ (*Volksgerichthof*)

Special Courts
• (*Sondergerichte*)

Source: Hilgemann, 1984

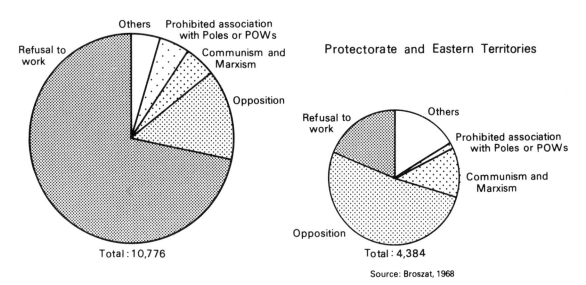

Fig. 3.21 Arrests by State Police

a broadly *völkisch* authoritarian tradition. However, such a body of law was fundamentally inconsistent with the precepts of National Socialism. The existence of a rigid and defined body of rules and precedents was inimical to a regime in which improvisation, arbitrariness and summary action were hallmarks.

Although the Nazis maintained a legal front in that there was no mass purge of the judiciary and much legal apparatus (e.g. in civil law) remained unchanged, they progressively undermined legality by the propagation of endless, often ill-defined new laws, by interfering in judicial matters, and, above all, by permitting and encouraging the growth of extra-legal organs like the Gestapo and the SS. The war signalled the watershed in this process. By 1943 there were over 40 crimes for which the death penalty was prescribed, whereas in 1933 there had been three. By the closing years of the war, Hitler was personally altering court sentences and judges were receiving regular guidelines from the Justice Ministry, making a mockery of any remaining judicial independence. But it was in the Nazi police state that the destruction of justice was most rapid. Summary arrests, the removal to concentration camps of prisoners decreed innocent in the courts, and SS execution squads were all features of a growing alternative basis of law in which the judiciary and its organs had less and less influence (Fig. 3.21). In some ways the courts became servants of the police, but in other respects they played no part at all, particularly as the racial ideology of Himmler's SS was pursued with ever-increasing zeal.

IV Part Four

Population and economy

26 Population

A persistent theme of Nazi propaganda was that Germany was a nation with an inadequate land area relative to the size of its population, enshrined in the slogan '*Volk ohne Raum*'. Most commonly this was conveyed by reciting the progressive shrinkage in the land area of Germany and its historical predecessors as far back as the Holy Roman Empire (Fig. 4.1). Another misleading device was to compare the population densities of world states with their colonial territories incorporated. In this manner, Germany came close to Japan and far ahead of any European state in the degree of its

Fig. 4.1 Der deutsche Staatsraum: contractions of the German state in history

Der deutsche Staatsraum

☐ The empire of Henry II (1180)

▨ The empire after the Thirty Years War (1648)

▥ Bismarck's empire (1871)

▢ Weimar Germany (1920)

Source: *Der nationalsozialistische Schulungsbrief*, 1938

'overcrowding'. However, the reality was quite otherwise. Germany's 69.6 million people resided on a larger *per capita* land area than either the British, Dutch or Belgian peoples; only against France was the comparison in any measure valid. What is more, the Nazi state took deliberate steps to raise the reproductive rate of its population. And by the late 1930s it was suffering a chronic shortage of able-bodied manpower. Thus have commentators been led to claim that Nazi Germany was a 'space without people', rather than a 'people without space'.

Except for the upward trend in the net reproduction rate, Nazi Germany exhibited most of the demographic features common to countries of Europe during the inter-war years (Figs. 4.2 and 4.3), namely a rising level of urbanisation, continuing rural-urban migration, a higher level of fertility in the countryside than in the towns, and a transfer within city regions from inner to outer suburbs. As is apparent from the accompanying map, extensive areas of Germany (with Austria and the Sudetenland) lost population between 1933 and 1939, notably in the rural east and south. The areas gaining population reflected the decisive programme of industrial expansion and resource development undertaken by the Nazi regime: for example, ship-building and all its ancillary industries at coastal centres on the North Sea and the Baltic; mining, metals, engineering, chemicals and agricultural processing in the belts centred on Hanover and Brunswick, and Leipzig and Dessau. Munich, Silesia and the Saar afford further examples. Most of the areas grew considerably from internal migration, as the map of migration balance reveals.

Fig. 4.2 Population change in Greater Germany, circa 1933–39

Fig. 4.3 Balance of migration, 1933-39

Balance of migration 1933-9

Gain		Loss
Over 8%		
4-8%		0-4%
0-4%		4-6%

Source: *Wirtschaft und Statistik,* 1940

Fig. 4.4 Birth rate in major German towns (Grossstädten), 1933 and 1937–41

Source: *Wirtschaft und Statistik,* 1941

The pattern of city growth between 1933 and 1939 echoes in many ways the general picture of population change (Fig. 4.4), even if some gains were attributable to boundary extensions. A selection of cities declined in population over the period, notably in the Ruhr (Gelsenkirchen, Duisburg-Hamborn, Dortmund, Oberhausen, Bochum) and in the former

Fig. 4.5 Age pyramid, 1938

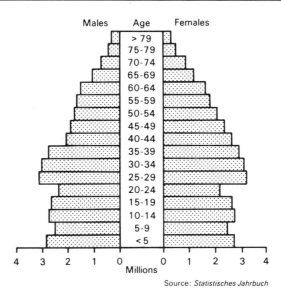

Source: *Statistisches Jahrbuch*

state of Saxony (Leipzig, Dresden, Chemnitz). Nowhere was the margin of decline greater than 6 per cent and it arose partly from out-of-town population movements. But in the case of the Ruhr, the pattern reflected a conscious policy to concentrate new industrial capacity away from the vulnerable border regions, and also the depressed state of the coal industry up to 1936.

Many of these demographic trends were quite contrary to Nazi policy goals. For example, the population losses in the eastern lands were in contradiction to the role cast for the farming peasantry there as the core of a renewed *volkisch* state. Urbanisation, in so far as it was typically correlated with lowering fertility, likewise ran counter to attempts by the Nazis to raise the German birth rate. However, there were features of the evolving demographic profile which, as viewed by ordinary Germans, acted in support of Nazi policies, even if in obviously specious ways. The falling birth rate cast shadows of *Volkstod*, the potential death of the nation, and thus lent justification not simply to pro-natal measures, but, more critically, to Jewish suppression. The fact that *Volkstod* was inconsistent with the slogan of '*Volk ohne Raum*' faded behind such racial overtones. The German demographic pyramid (Fig. 4.5) also lent a strangely plausible justification for Nazi policy goals. The Weimar years were characterised by a bulging younger generation: those born into the decade up to the Great War. Many of this generation came on to the labour market as economic conditions were in decline. They became a surplus population and so looked favourably upon measures which offered their lives direction and reward. Here the notion of competition for living space had an immediate meaning, whatever its wider inconsistencies. Another feature of the demographic pyramid was the greater number of women in the middle cohorts. Barred from marriage and motherhood by the absence of sufficient men, the surplus women helped to swell the emancipatory tide towards greater female participation in the labour market, but in the process adding fuel to policies which sought to

Source: Kulischer, 1943

Fig. 4.6 Transfer of German minorities, 1939–42

enhance the maternal role, especially in times of high male unemployment.

The war naturally brought with it radical and sometimes abrupt changes in Germany's demographic characteristics. The birth rate held up in the first 18 months of war, but thereafter it fell. In 1942, the total was 14.9 per thousand, almost back to the level of 1933. As the war progressed, there was a rising number of deaths among civilians due to enemy bombardment. By May 1945, the cumulative total was 650,000, not far short of the average for the annual number of deaths in Germany in the 1930s. In geographical terms, however, the most significant demographic changes occurred in migration. Civilian workers were compulsorily transferred to meet specific labour shortages. Territorial expansion involved vast movements in the military population and all their supporting civilian personnel. German minorities totalling over half a million in the Baltic states (Lithuania, Latvia and Estonia), Poland, eastern Rumania and South Tyrol were resettled in Greater Germany (Fig. 4.6). Europe's Jews were progressively rooted out and forcibly transported to the concentration and death camps in the eastern territories. Then, as Hitler's empire was forced to contract in the face of Allied advance, the scale and intensity of migration increased further. By early 1945, it was dominated by the westward flight of Germans in the path of the advancing Red Army.

27 | *Agriculture and food supply*

Any examination of agriculture and, more especially, food supply in Nazi Germany has to accommodate the special problems posed by world markets under the forces of depression and also the variabilities of climate over northern and central Europe (Figs. 4.7 and 4.8). The room for manoeuvre in setting out a determinedly National Socialist agrarian policy and the problem of meeting production targets were both considerably circumscribed by these twin features. For several decades before Hitler's accession, protectionism in agriculture had been a familiar cry, for a host of different reasons. The world depression pushed Germany further along the path of agricultural autarky as the country's exporting potential was curtailed and the capacity for food imports was reduced in turn. Throughout the 1930s, Germany suffered a persistent shortage of foreign currency, making large-scale foreign food imports impossible. And to complicate the position, Nazi re-armament policies made increasing demands on the meagre foreign currency reserves in the purchase of industrial raw materials like quality iron ore not found within the Reich's borders. Thus when the National Socialists declared their intentions towards a more self-sufficient agriculture, particularly in the long-standing deficit area of fats, they were responding as much to force of circumstance and traditional predisposition as to any preferred policy, for all that policy was consistent with their war aims. Moreover, the force of circumstance took a new twist in 1934 following a disastrous harvest season. This prompted the setting up of the 'Battle of Production', in which the acreage under grain was to be reduced, but the quantity of grain maintained and the released land then made over to fodder cultivation. However, the

Fig. 4.7 Volume index of agricultural production (1927–29 = 100)

140
120
100
80
60
40
20
0

1932/3   1934/5   1936/7   1938/9

Note: Excluding share due to fodder   Source: Klein, 1959

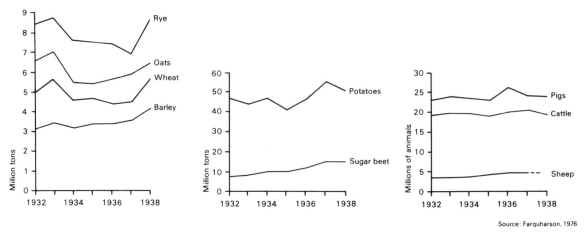

Fig. 4.8 Agricultural production and stockholding: 1932–38

scheme soon ran into difficulties, most of them triggered by another poor harvest in 1935.

Farm incomes, by contrast, did not tell so grim a story in the first years of the Nazi regime. Much of the agrarian sector saw a growing surplus. In 1932–3, the excess of sales over expenses had fallen to 0.5 billion Reichmarks. By 1934–5, it had risen to 2.3 billion Reichmarks with the aid of higher prices, debt relief measures and tax cuts. Unfortunately, the pattern was not maintained for long.

New measures for agricultural production were introduced in 1936 under Goering's Four-Year-Plan organisation. These included reductions in fertiliser prices, mechanisation subsidies and grants for bringing new land under cultivation. The results were measurably favourable, assisted by a

Fig. 4.9 Land sown with fodder and fibre-bearing plants (thousand ha)

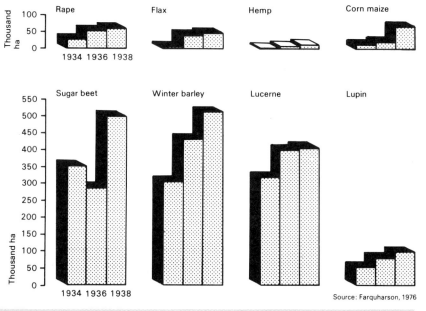

Source: Farquharson, 1976

Fig. 4.10 Self-sufficiency in important foodstuffs, 1938–39

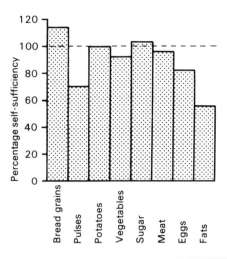

Source: Noakes and Pridham, 1984

good harvest year in 1938 and again in 1939. By 1938/9, farm production was some 20 per cent up on the figure for 1928/9. Fodder areas had grown substantially (Fig. 4.9). There was also an increase in food consumption per head of population of about 4 to 5 per cent. But still by 1938/9, the country was able to meet only 57 per cent of its fats demand (Fig. 4.10). This was only a four-point rise on 1933/4. Indeed, it was half the corresponding rise between 1927/8 and 1933/4 (nine points). The explanation was that the provisions of the Four-Year-Plan had been heavily biased towards arable rather than livestock farming (Fig. 4.11). In 1938/9, 43 per cent of livestock feed was still imported, the unit costs of which had been steadily rising on the world market. Thus compared with their arable counterparts, livestock farmers benefited from few subsidies and faced rising costs for items such as

Fig. 4.11 Agricultural yields in 1933, 1939 and 1944 (per hectare; in double zentner)

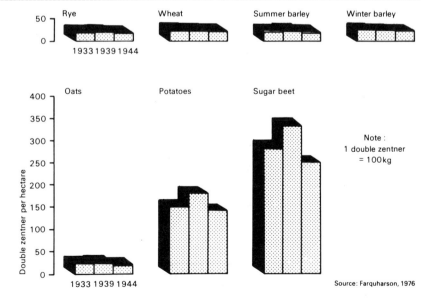

Note :
1 double zentner
= 100 kg

Source: Farquharson, 1976

farm housing and machinery at a time when agricultural prices were effectively frozen by the Reich Food Estate. This was not the sum total of the policy failures, though. For behind improvements in other food sectors there lay a basic growing weakness; the flight from the land. Between 1933 and 1939, agriculture may have lost up to half a million people, and most of the measures that the Nazis introduced to stem the flow actually intensified it in the longer term.

The onset of war conditions magnified the many problems of National Socialist agriculture. Trade blockade brought a drastic decline in fodder imports and in essential fertilisers like potash. Labour loss intensified such that women, juveniles and foreign workers were being engaged in increasing numbers by the middle of the war. And despite the pre-existence of a central co-ordination and planning body in the form of the Reich Food Estate, a variety of factors (not least the conflicting power blocks in the Third Reich) impeded a full-scale direction of agriculture.

28 *Raw materials and industry*

Germany's industrial machine underwent a traumatic decline during the Depression (Fig. 4.12). In some sectors, production fell by around 70 per cent over the years 1929 to 1931. It was partly the depth of this crisis that prompted business leaders to put their support behind National Socialism in 1933, quite aside from any benefits that they perceived from a renewed political hegemony which might help to maintain the existing structures of capital. The first pre-occupation under Nazi rule was simple regeneration of industrial capacity and industrial investment (Fig. 4.13). In fact, it took until around 1935/6 to achieve the levels of production of the pre-Depression

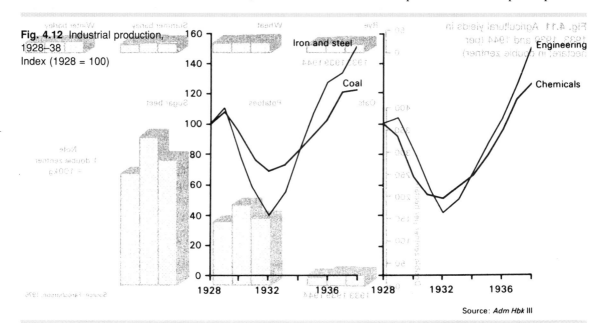

Fig. 4.12 Industrial production, 1928–38
Index (1928 = 100)

Source: *Adm Hbk* III

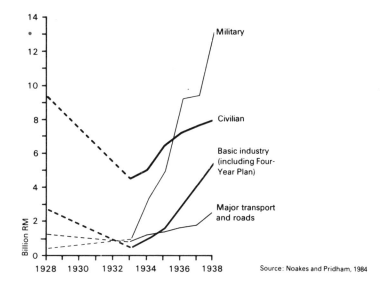

Fig. 4.13 Estimated economic investment, 1933–38

Military

Civilian

Basic industry (including Four-Year Plan)

Major transport and roads

Billion RM

1928 1930 1932 1934 1936 1938

Source: Noakes and Pridham, 1984

years. This was not the sum total of the Depression's effects, though. As in agriculture, the deficient state of the country's export earnings capacity placed severe limits on imports of industrial raw materials and goods. Foreign currency reserves were small and had to be strictly rationed. Again in common with agriculture, therefore, a policy of autarky was set. The primary vehicle was Goering's Four-Year-Plan Organisation with its exceptional room for intervention in economic administration. Three materials were singled out in particular: iron ore, oil and rubber.

In the later 1930s, Germany was second only to the USA as a world producer of iron and steel. However, such dominance was not based on German ores. The country had extensive ore deposits (Fig. 4.14) but these were mostly poor in quality, some with iron contents of only 20 to 30 per cent. Thus the bulk of Germany's ore came from outside, particularly from Sweden where iron content was normally around 60 per cent. Goering's scheme was to expand substantially the exploitation of home ores, notably those from the Salzgitter field in Hanover. For this purpose, an industrial corporation, the Hermann Goering Ore and Foundry Company, was established. Ore production was scheduled to rise to 24 million tons by 1944, whereas at the time of the corporation's establishment the Salzgitter field yielded less than a million tons. There was to be a parallel though lesser-scale development of ore-fields in Franconia in the south, and in both mining areas iron and steel plants were to be erected on site, bringing in coking coal from the Ruhr. The whole scheme was patently uneconomic, but the Nazi leadership saw this as immaterial given the reduced reliance on foreign ores and the strategic gain of a dispersion in iron and steel capacity. In practice, ore extraction and iron and steel capacity never matched anything like that envisaged in the scheme. Ore production from the Salzgitter field, for instance, was only 4.2 million tons in 1942, while the Franconian iron and steel plant never materialised at all. The reasons for this were various, some highly specific but others more ill-defined. The territorial expansion of the Third Reich, beginning with Austrian annexation in 1938,

Fig. 4.14 Iron ore workings, 1937

Iron ore workings
1937

Iron ore output
(million tons)

● 0.8-1.0
● 0.1-0.4
• Under 0.1
▣ Cities

Source: *Adm Hbk* III

brought with it ore supplies of better quality and augmented iron and steel capacity on a very substantial scale, especially with the conquest of France and the Benelux countries in 1940. The speed of success of Hitler's Blitzkrieg operations rapidly undermined the rationale behind domestic exploitation and development. Similarly significant, though, was the manner in which the Goering industrial enterprise grew. Like so many organisations of the *Hitler state*, it developed a force and momentum of its own, becoming a massive, almost capitalistic, industrial conglomerate through new development, partnership and amalgamation, particularly in occupied territories, and bearing increasingly little relation to the aims of the Four-Year-Plan Organisation under which it was born.

A somewhat similar story was presented in oil production. The Four-Year-Plan instituted a battery of measures to advance the production of mineral oil, including high tariffs on imported oil. In parallel, the production of synthetic oil (from coal and lignite) was to be radically expanded (Fig. 4.15). However, the plan targets were not met. In 1939 production of mineral and synthetic oil was around 40 per cent below the level intended. In 1940 it was 20 per cent below. Production performance was better in mineral than in synthetic oil, where the enormous manpower and transport requirements for a process using 5 to 6 tons of coal to produce one ton of oil made real difficulties.

Rubber production, by contrast, was one area of the Four-Year-Plan where the target was more nearly approached. In the mid-1930s, Germany had the largest rubber industry of continental Europe, based on imported

Fig. 4.15 Synthetic production of raw materials

The largely unavoidable concentration of the Fischer–Tropsch oil capacity (using coal and coke) in the Ruhr was to prove a serious liability in the face of the Allied bombing campaign from 1943.

natural rubber. The plan aimed to reduce this import dependency by developing the manufacture of synthetic rubber (Buna) from acetylene (Fig. 4.15). A pilot plant already existed at Leverkusen. The plan envisaged the establishment of three major production plants, the first of them at Schkopau near Leipzig. By the outbreak of war, synthetic rubber production was 22,000 tons per annum, as against a natural output approaching 100,000

Fig. 4.16 Militarisation of
IG-Farben's investments,
1932–44

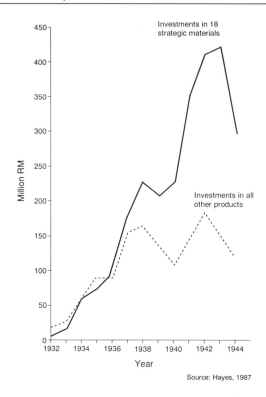

Source: Hayes, 1987

tons. By late 1943, nine synthetic plants were producing almost 100,000 tons annually, which met consumption needs in broad terms.

The programme of synthetic production was spearheaded by the giant chemicals firm IG-Farben. By 1930, it constituted not only the largest industrial combine in Europe, but the fourth largest in the world. It embraced 50 semi-autonomous independent firms, while the core firm alone boasted more than 100 plants and mines. Karl Krauch, a senior member of its board, had been appointed to the Four-Year-Plan Organisation from its inception in 1936 and from 1938 became General Plenipotentiary for Chemicals. This meant that he exercised full control over the planning and production of synthetics, a position of inestimable value to IG-Farben as a near-monopolist in the German chemical sector. This form of alliance between an organisation of the Nazi state and a leading empire of private industrial capital became typical as the regime moved to a war footing (Fig. 4.16). It was the most expedient way of achieving a given production objective. IG-Farben saw its business profits describe a quantum leap (Fig. 4.17), although its direct contribution to Nazi Party funds did not rise as impressively. The records of other firms were less spectacular, but in 1939, undistributed profits of limited liability companies were four times higher than in 1928.

The particular nature of the relationship between the Nazi state and firms like IG-Farben was for a long while one of the most potent points of controversy in interpretations of the Third Reich. In some ways it has now become a caricature to say that it reflected an argument between the

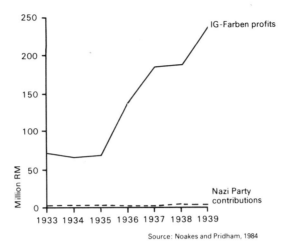

Fig. 4.17 Net profits of the IG-Farben Combine, 1933–39

Source: Noakes and Pridham, 1984

'primacy of politics' on the one hand and the 'primacy of economics' on the other, but this sets out the points of reference unambiguously. In the former case, business interests were construed as thoroughly subservient to the political leadership; in the latter, the Nazi state functioned simply as an agency for organised capital. Modern opinion is more doubtful of the value of the concept of primacy and of the demarcation between state and private economic interests that its use has invited. It is suggested, too, that not only was the disposition of power more fractured, but it was also much more prone to flux as the Third Reich ran its tortuous course. One might conclude by saying that the political leadership and private business found common interests which brought them into various forms of structural alliance. But the unfolding of events, in peace and in war, periodically affected the balance of these interests, in cases propelling them in directions which became mutually antagonistic – a feature that became decisive in the final years of the war.

29 *Re-armament*

Alongside the drive for self-sufficiency in raw materials, the key feature of industrial manufacture in Nazi Germany was re-armament, embracing a whole range of production sectors. In 1932 Germany spent only 1 per cent of its gross national product on defence and armament. By 1939, the figure had risen to nearly a quarter. Measured against public investment alone, military spending reached 74 per cent of the total in 1938. The making of armoured vehicles, weaponry and munitions, together with naval building, defensive fortification and the development of the Luftwaffe, all placed heavy demands upon Germany's productive capacity (Fig. 4.18). It is estimated that investment in this sector grew from 1 billion Reichsmarks in 1933 to 13.6 billion in 1938, with much of it concentrated in the north and west. From 1934 the Reichsbank was issuing extensive credits to assist production expansion in those firms engaged in armaments contracts. Industrial invest-

Fig. 4.18 Main sulphuric acid plants in Germany: circa 1937–38. The map shows plants with a capacity of 20,000 tons per annum. Sulphuric acid was vital to the production of explosives and forms a fundamental base to chemical industries generally. In 1937, the Lower Rhine area contributed nearly 43 per cent of sulphuric acid production

ment, much of which was directly and indirectly tied to military demands, grew from 0.5 billion Reichsmarks in 1933 to 5.6 billion Reichsmarks in 1938. This included the synthetic programmes of the Four-Year-Plan and the mining of low-grade metals (Fig. 4.19). The manufacturing sector that proved most inadequate in meeting the requirements placed on it was steel. The problem was that, aside from the Hermann Goering enterprises, little new steel-making capacity was added under Nazi rule. There was also a persistent weakness in the priority allocation of steels, demands from sectors entirely extraneous to re-armament often absorbing valuable output. Labour for all this expanded industrial production was drawn largely from the ranks

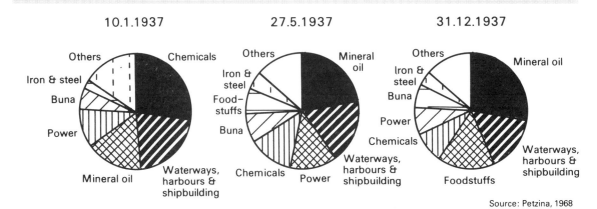

Fig. 4.19 Distribution of investment in organisation of the Four-Year-Plan, 1937

of the unemployed, their number falling from around 6 million in early 1933 to around 1 million by late 1936. This meant that there was no fundamental redirection of labour within the German economy. There was some out-movement from agricultural occupations, but the production of consumer goods, for example, was not greatly affected by re-armament. Consumer goods production showed consistent growth throughout the peacetime years of National Socialism. In fact, there was a determination on the part of Nazi leaders not to force civilian sacrifices. To reiterate a common contemporary expression: many, not all, Germans under Hitler had both guns and butter, though at the cost of a rapidly rising public debt.

Any assessment of National Socialism's relationship with the control and organisation of industry and business, must be set against the background of a relatively highly organised pattern of economic life well before 1933. And aside from the creation of such bodies as the Four-Year-Plan organisation, the Nazi accession mostly witnessed a consolidation of this pattern. Membership of the former widely representative trade associations became compulsory, for instance, and the *Führerprinzip* was established within them. The largest of these was that for industry and this remained so from 1933. The *Reichsgruppe for Industry* had seven functional sub-divisions and each subdivision was further subdivided. The general label the Nazis used to describe this form of organisation was 'self-administration', but the only real sense in which this applied was in terms of personnel. Industrial administration was carried out by industrialists, not civil servants, but nevertheless under direct state supervision.

Before 1933, Germany also had a comprehensive industrial and business organisation in the field, that is a distinctive geographical organisation. Indeed, membership of a local Chamber of Industry and Commerce had been compulsory for all firms. The Chambers were staffed through democratic election among their members, and there were statutory regulations providing for consultation between the Chambers and central government departments. The Nazis largely confirmed this organisational pattern, except that the *Führerprinzip*, that is control from the top, was substituted for the previous democratic arrangement. There were 111 separate Chambers and this remained so until 1942 when the number was reduced to 42 to bring them into line with the party Gaue.

30 *Transport and communications*

The autobahn programme

Of all the measures instituted by the National Socialists, the autobahn programme must have been among the most positive. Indeed, the autobahn system remains today as one of the few lasting reminders of Hitler's Germany. The concept of the high-speed motor-road with separate carriageways and limited access points had already been employed in Berlin and, on a larger scale, in Italy and the USA. In Nazi Germany, however, the

Fig. 4.20 Investment in roads
and railways, 1925–38

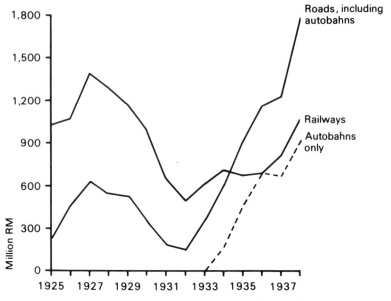

Sources: *Statistisches Jahrbuch,*
Statistisches Handbuch

Fig. 4.21 Autobahns, early 1939

concept was carried forward on an even more comprehensive scale and at a more rapid rate. Within five years of the programme's inception some 3,000 kilometres of road were open, another 1,500 kilometres were under construction, and a further 2,400 kilometres were authorised (Figs. 4.20 and 4.21). For its time, the autobahn programme represented a highly advanced engineering venture in which many of the latest techniques of civil engineering were applied, particularly in surface construction and finish, and in the large-scale use of concrete. It provides one of the many cases in Nazi Germany where the use of advanced scientific technology rested side by side with pseudo-science as practised in the regime's racial and eugenic policies.

The objectives of the autobahn programme were at once political, economic and strategic. In January 1933, the total number of unemployed had topped 6 million. A major road-building programme offered a way of absorbing some of that figure. By late 1934, some 350,000 people were directly and indirectly employed in it. The geographical configuration of the autobahn system in part reflected the internal trade demands of a well-developed industrial economy, witnessed in the early completion of the links between the major ports of Bremen, Hamburg and Lübeck, and those joining the north-west industrial region based on the Ruhr with the central industrial belt extending from Hanover through Leipzig to Dresden. As the map reveals, however, the planned network looked outward from the country's border regions as much as it sought to bind internal elements of it: for instance in the southward extensions from Nuremberg and Munich and in the eastward thrusts from Breslau and Bayreuth. All these had strategic significance in a military sense, although army leaders favoured railway rather than road transport. Nuremberg's position in the network was also justified in terms of its being the site of the annual Nazi Party rally.

The rapid progress of the autobahn system owed much to the Supreme Reich Authority under the direction of Fritz Todt. Outside of ministerial jurisdictions, and yet with powers to initiate legislation and to issue administrative decrees, Todt was able to devise a form of organisation geared specially to his road-building task and to marshal private and public enterprise accordingly. Much as Goering in his capacity as chief of the Four-Year-Plan Organisation, Todt enjoyed an element of direct Führer authority and exercised it widely. He went on to organise conscripted and slave labour for construction projects across occupied Europe. By November 1944, the *Organisation Todt* had a workforce numbering over 1.25 million.

The Reichsbahn

Nazi Germany possessed one of the largest European railway systems (Fig. 4.22). Its 54,000 kilometre length was exceeded only by the USSR. In terms of network density and mileage per head of population, it equated closely with the United Kingdom. The fairly wide availability of coal for locomotive fuel and the relatively wide spread of industrial and other economic foci made German railway operation a profitable business. Germany's geographical position at the centre of Europe reinforced this in terms of the opportunities for cross-border passenger and freight traffic.

The German state had a long tradition of involvement in the railways. By

Fig. 4.22 The railway network, 1938

1910, Prussia, for instance, owned some 98 per cent of its lines following a policy of state acquisition extending over 30 years. Under the Weimar constitution, the entire German railway system came under state control, but the subsequent collapse of the currency enforced a largely independent management structure for the railways, notably in budgetary terms. The working profits of the railways then became one of the principal sources of reparation repayments. By the early 1930s, the German railways' revenues were again their own, and by 1937 the Nazis had co-ordinated the system in the service of the state through the fusion of the duties of railways chief and Minister of Transport.

Despite the formidable transport facility represented by the railway system, the story of its relations with National Socialism is one characterised by lagging investment, strategic oversight and jurisdictional inefficiencies. From the beginning the railway system was cast in the shadow of Todt's great autobahn programme. And in some Nazi quarters, railways were viewed as *passé*, to be superseded by the growth of motor and air transport. The vast scale of the railway administrative organisation (Fig. 4.23) also

Fig. 4.23 Regions of railway administration, 1938

H	Hamburg
Sw	Schwerin
Sn	Stettin
Ks	Königsberg
Ms	Münster
Hn	Hanover
B	Berlin
Fo	Frankfurt-an-der-Oder
E	Essen
Kl	Kassel
Ha	Halle
Dr	Dresden
Bs	Breslau
Op	Oppein
C	Cologne
W	Wuppertal-am-Main
Er	Erfurt
Sr	Saarbrücken
Mz	Mainz
N	Nuremberg
Kr	Karlsruhe
S	Stuttgart
A	Augsburg
M	Munich
Rn	Regensburg

Regions of railway administration 1938

0   200 km

Source: *Adm Hbk* IV   Note: Boundaries are only schematic

generated antipathy in Nazi officialdom. Much as the civil service was distrusted by Hitler and his leaders, so too was the railway administration. It had a too wide and too deeply rooted power base. Moreover, the almost complete lack of coincidence between the railway administrative regions (*Reichsbahndirektionen*) and the party Gaue intensified difficulties. The railway director at Frankfurt-am-Main, for instance, had to deal with six different Gauleiters.

The paradox was that by the late 1930s, effective demand for rail transportation was greater than it had ever been. Conditions of economic boom, the refortification schemes in the west and the army's growing requirements combined to intensify pressure on the system. In 1938, there were difficulties moving the coal mined. By 1939, passenger trains were increasingly subject to sudden cancellation. Electrification schemes in progress on some routes added to the problems.

The Nazi attitude to railways was reflected in their very limited use of them in the reoccupation of the Rhineland and in the annexation of Austria. In fact, the regime entered into war with no proper plans for the railways, either in strategic or investment terms. The railway system was soon under intense strain. There were shortages of manpower and machines, and there was a minimum of centralised co-ordination in the service of war. Even greater strains were imposed as territorial conquests accumulated. By December 1941 some 15,000 kilometres of broad-gauge track in Russia had been converted to standard gauge, but this had needed 70,000 men from the Reichsbahn organisation. No special locomotive production programme was introduced until late 1941. Only then, under the organising impetus of Armaments Minister Speer, was a standard wartime locomotive class commissioned. Later, Speer set up a production organisation for motive power and stock which was separate from the Reichsbahn.

As the Reichsbahn attempted to meet the diverse demands of transporting men, materials and the victims of Himmler's death camps, as the various power groupings of the Third Reich fought bitterly over railway capacity,

Hitler was busy planning a super broad-gauge railway consistent with his monumental dreams for the thousand-year Reich.

Aviation

The Versailles Treaty had forbidden the construction of aircraft for military purposes, but there was no slackening in the pace of German investment in civil aircraft development; this laid the foundation for a vigorous civil aviation industry by the early 1930s, heavily backed by successive German governments. National Socialist policy was to extend this pattern, as witnessed in the foundation of an Air Ministry headed by Goering within months of Hitler's chancellorship and by increasing levels of state subsidy, often in excess of regular commercial demands. The expansion of the civil sector, particularly the technical research and development that accompanied it, was an obvious springboard for the reinstatement of a combat air force. Thus, when Hitler announced the beginning of air rearmament in March 1935, a vigorous Luftwaffe was not long in creation.

From the mid-1920s, civil air services became the monopoly of one company, Deutsche Lufthansa, and by 1937 it operated directly some 76 routes and maintained interests in many others (Fig. 4.24). In 1939, 50 per

Fig. 4.24 Principal routes of Deutsche Lufthansa, 1937

Principal routes
of Deutsche Lufthansa
1937

Numbers of passengers carried

2,000
10,000
25,000

Borders as in 1937

Note: Some routes include intermediate stops

Source: *Adm Hbk* IV

cent of the company's revenue came from direct subsidy, 35 per cent from passengers and 15 per cent from cargo and mail.

The Nazis used aviation to boost their progressive image in much the same fashion as they used the autobahn programme. Hitler became a frequent air traveller, a pattern instituted by Goebbels as a symbolic means of reinforcing the *Führer*'s overarching appeal to the German nation. The supreme irony of this later on in the war was that Hitler forbade his senior military commanders to travel by air because of the enemy risk. Thus Rommel was a critical 10 hours in getting from his home in Germany to command the Normandy defence against the Allied landings on 6 June 1944.

Radio broadcasting

The importance of radio to the Nazi dictatorship hardly needs to be emphasised. The German state held a broadcasting monopoly long before Hitler, as indeed was the case in Britain. There were sound operational reasons for national control of broadcasting, quite aside from matters of government stability. But in the hands of a regime seeking to radicalise or overturn existing practices and institutions of the state, of course, radio was a devastatingly effective medium. The Nazi Propaganda Ministry was quick to appreciate this and programming was soon rigorously systematised in the service of Nazism. In parallel, the mass production of cheap radio receivers became a priority, with the result that the number of households with access to a receiver rose from 4.5 million in early 1933 to 16 million by the middle of the war (Fig. 4.25). Nazi Germany soon had the densest radio receiver coverage in the world (Fig. 4.26).

Fig. 4.25 Number of radio/ wireless receivers per 100 households, 1929–41 (Altreich only)

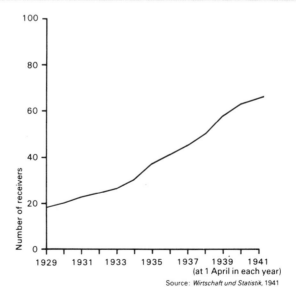

Source: *Wirtschaft und Statistik*, 1941

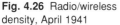

Fig. 4.26 Radio/wireless density, April 1941

31   *Trade and trade policy*

The nature and course of Nazi trade policy are not themes which lend themselves to simple interpretation. For example, there was no fundamental discontinuity between the policies of the later Weimar administrations and those of Hitler. In large part, this reflected the basic facts of German economic life before, during and immediately after the Depression. A deeper problem, though, centres upon the longer term goals of Nazi trade policy. Was the policy mainly a response to evolving economic expediencies? Or did it embrace dimensions of Nazi ideology, including the extension of German living space in eastern Europe?

German foreign trade declined dramatically over the years of the Depression and stagnated throughout the 1930s (Fig. 4.27). The country was continually short of foreign exchange for the imports of food, textiles and industrial raw materials, and exports required subsidy in the face of declining world prices. However, up to 1936/7, the price of most of the commodities imported fell much faster than the prices of Germany's characteristic exports. As the adjacent graphs show, the *volume* of imports (i.e. imports at fixed prices, 1928) held up relatively well, given the severity of the world depression. This was of vital importance for the foodstuffs sector and for the expansion of the armaments industry.

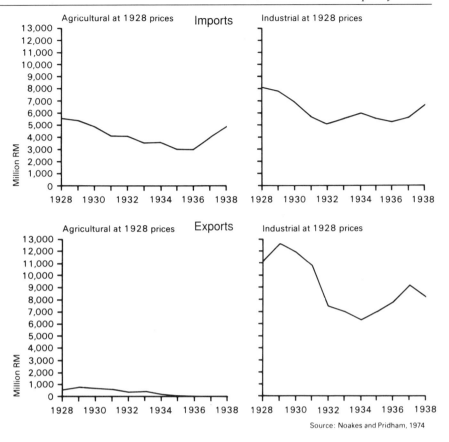

Source: Noakes and Pridham, 1974

Fig. 4.27 Visible trade imports and exports, 1928–38

In the supply of industrial raw materials, as well as of foodstuffs, National Socialism sought import substitution or autarky. But the scale of the expansion in the armaments and related industries was well beyond the country's substitution capacity and thus the trend was for an increasing proportion of imports to be taken up by industrial raw materials. In 1932, they formed some 27 per cent of imports by value. By 1936, the figure had risen to just over 37. Food imports dropped from around 46 per cent to 35 per cent in the corresponding period. However, the trends were not sustained, for in the closing years of peace the gap narrowed once more. Even so, it is impossible to escape the way imports such as iron ore grew in magnitude. Between 1935 and 1937 the total rose from 14 to 21 million tons, roughly half coming from the rich Swedish fields.

The debate over the goals of Nazi Germany's 'autarkic' trade policy is a difficult one. The crisis of world capitalist organisation from 1929 to 1932 and the haunting lessons of food supply during the First World War undoubtedly struck their own path towards autarky, in agriculture as well as in industry. But some commentators have seen the policy in a much more positive light, as part of a deliberate plan by Hitler, aimed among other things, at rearmament. A variant of this interpretation argues that rearmament itself

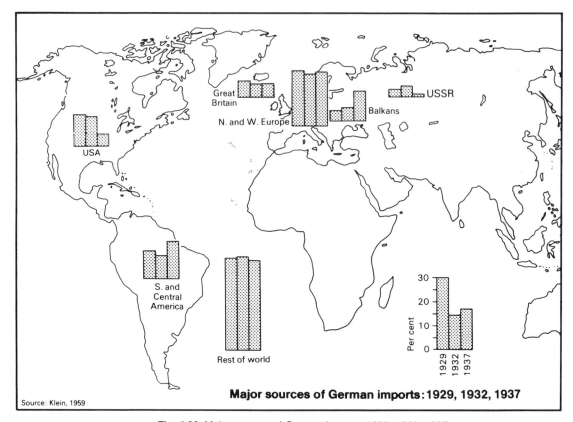

Fig. 4.28 Major sources of German imports: 1929, 1932, 1937

was a primary driving force towards autarky in terms of the pressures that it placed on currency reserves and the severe political repercussions of any deceleration in the arms industry's expansion.

Under National Socialism, Germany also saw a re-orientation of primary trading partners (Fig. 4.28), involving an expansion of dealings with the Balkans and South and Central America, and a reduction of dealings with former partners such as the United States. The policy had its origins in the last administrations of the Weimar regime when foreign trade with Western Europe (including Great Britain) and the United States became difficult, largely due to the relative uncompetitiveness of German export goods as a consequence of an overvalued mark. The solution took the form of bilateral trading agreements with countries such as Yugoslavia, Rumania and Hungary (most of whom found themselves similarly placed to Germany), transactions essentially being carried out on a barter basis. Germany exported to these Balkan states a range of manufactured goods and imported vital raw materials like chrome, bauxite and oil. The National Socialists took up this foreign trade policy and reinforced it. Similiar trade agreements were forged with countries of Latin America, and, with the added facility of an increasingly centralised regulation of the dealings of German importers and exporters, National Socialism was able to apply considerable leverage on its bilateral trade partners.

Fig. 4.29 Countries with more than 10 per cent of their exports taken by Germany in 1937

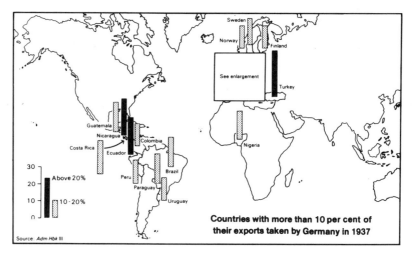

Countries with more than 10 per cent of their exports taken by Germany in 1937

Source: *Adm Hbk* III

Countries with more than 10 per cent of their exports taken by Germany in 1937

Source: *Adm Hbk* III

The accompanying diagrams (Fig. 4.29) illustrate the substance of these various changes. By 1937, the Balkans and Latin America were supplying some 28 per cent of German imports by value, whereas in 1929 they had supplied only 15. Bulgaria had 43 per cent of its exports (by value) taken by Germany, Turkey 36 per cent, and Greece 31 per cent. In certain of these countries, Germany ran an import surplus, thereby underscoring the degree of their dependence.

The strategic dimensions of this evolving trade policy require little elucidation. Trade sources in south-east Europe were not liable to blockade in the event of war, while the political allegiances of Latin Amercian states were as likely to be neutral or pro-German as they were to be pro-western. These various merits were soon to reveal themselves as Hitler embarked upon his plans for territorial annexation, ultimately taking Germany into world war.

V Part Five

The search for living space: the Third Reich at war

32 *Territorial annexation*

National Socialist foreign policy does not lend itself to simple explanation. The facts of territorial acquisition and aggression may be incontrovertible but the reasons behind them have long been a seat of argument. Some have seen Nazi foreign policy as continuing trends which characterised the Weimar and Wilhelmine eras, particularly in the desire for eastward territorial extension. Some consider that anti-communism was the central driving force behind Nazi policy; others that it was fired by racialism and the desire for Aryan hegemony in Europe and, later, in the world. But the most difficult controversy is that embracing the *functionalist* and *intentionalist* interpretations of events and actions. The latter sees Nazi foreign policy as the outcome of deliberate plans and ideas, not necessarily rigid, but embodying certain defined goals and illustrating some internal logic. The former sees Nazi policy as mainly articulated by forces acting upon the leadership. In other words, the stage for Hitler's actions was circumscribed by the evolving relations and political positions of the European states; in this way Hitler emerges as something of an opportunist. Events at home may be examined in a similar manner. It has been argued, for example, that the drive for additional territory in 1938–9 was powered by a growing internal economic crisis which only new lands and new resources could ameliorate. The foreign policy sequence may also, in the short term, reflect the power struggle of Ribbentrop's foreign office organisation as it vied not only with other Nazi power groupings, but with the established German Foreign Office and its career diplomats.

At first, Hitler's activities appeared to be concerned primarily with the reversal of the Versailles Treaty's provisions and of the incorporation in the Reich of lands inhabited by ethnic Germans. Thus was the Rhineland remilitarised, Austria seized, the Czech Sudetenland absorbed and Memel occupied (the Saarland became part of Germany by choice). But when Nazi policy became directed towards the subjugation of the entire Czechoslovak state, consisting of mainly non-German peoples, the picture also became one of militarist expansionism. The strike against Poland which marked the beginning of the Second World War, confirmed the later pattern.

Fig. 5.1 Territorial
annexation, 1935–39

The scale of Germany's territorial acquisitions in 1938 and early 1939
was vast (Fig. 5.1). By the time of the incorporation of the Sudetenland, the
Altreich had been augmented in area by roughly a quarter and its population
by about one-sixth. The Saar, Austria and the Sudetenland contained in 1938

approximately 11.3 million inhabitants. But the real significance of the extended Reich lay in the industrial raw materials and manufacturing capacity that it brought. Austria had important resources of iron ore and lignite. In the Sudetenland, valuable coal and lignite deposits were acquired, while Bohemia and Moravia provided armaments works, iron and steel plants, chemical and engineering factories, as well as coal, lignite and wood. The first annexations also made the next conquests much easier, although their sequence was not planned for this reason.

33   *Territorial conquest*

Although the Second World War is usually said to have begun on 3 September 1939, following upon Germany's invasion of Poland two days earlier, it fell short of being a 'world' war for some two years. Indeed, for almost a year it became for the British a 'phoney' war and for their German counterparts a 'Sitzkrieg'. The first British bombs on Berlin fell on 25 August 1940, for instance. Initially, it was not even a war in which a majority of European states was embroiled. Italian support for Germany was not immediately forthcoming. Literally days before the Polish invasion, Hitler had secured a non-aggression pact with Russia. Some countries, Sweden and Spain among them, never entered the war at all. It began as a world war only in so far as British colonies and dominions described a worldwide distribution and in so far as these interests became an immediate target for surface and submarine raiders.

The prosecution of the war was also distinctive. Gone was the dogged attrition of men which so characterised trench warfare. In its place, the Germans introduced 'Blitzkrieg': 'lightning war'. There were three central themes to its strategy: surprise; rapid mobility of forces; and the crippling of the enemy by cutting supply and control lines. The Polish invasion saw 'Blitzkrieg' in operation for the first time and it proved a resounding success. The Polish air force was destroyed in two days, the Polish army as a viable fighting unit within a week, reeling under the isolating effects of two pincer movements by the German forces. Poland's fate was finally sealed by the entry of the Russian army on to Polish soil in accordance with a secret plan agreed at the time of the German–Soviet non-aggression pact a few weeks previously. At the end of September, Poland was partitioned, the western half going to Germany, the eastern to Russia (Fig. 5.2).

Germany's military success was in part explained by Poland's military weakness, the bulk of the latter's forces consisting of immobile, unmotorised infantry. But the tactical advantages of 'Blitzkrieg', particularly in a relatively flat country like Poland, with vulnerable borders all round, were enormous. In the process, Poland became a formidable proving ground for modern tank warfare and for the German Panzers in particular.

'Blitzkrieg' also had a significance which extended far beyond the realm of the military tactician. It required only a limited economic commitment to war. The short, sharp shock of 'Blitzkrieg' needed armament in breadth not in depth. This meant a wide, highly efficient range of air and ground forces,

Fig. 5.2 Polish partition

but with only limited capacity for replacement. Rapid conquest rendered armament in depth unnecessary. This pattern of war economy remained a crucial dimension of Nazi Germany for a little over two years, although as much the product of circumstance as design. It was the first winter of the Russian campaign, in November 1941, that finally exposed its weaknesses.

With the liquidation of Poland, Hitler turned his attention to the west, although not until he had made an abortive effort to secure peace, notably with Britain. Plans for a lightning invasion of the Low Countries (Benelux) and France were slow to be formulated; execution in fact waited until the late spring of 1940, prior to which Hitler had moved to secure Germany's northern flank by occupying Denmark and Norway. The campaign in the west was just as successful as that in the east (Fig. 5.3). The Netherlands capitulated within five days, Belgium in eight, and France in six weeks. The Germans succeeded in splitting the Allied forces and Britain was forced to engage in a risky though highly successful evacuation of Allied troops seaward from Dunkirk. Under the Armistice signed with the French on 22 June 1940, Germany occupied a large part of France, including the entire northern and western coasts. In the remainder, a collaborationist French government was established at Vichy (Fig. 5.4).

By mid-summer 1940, Hitler's Germany embraced a vast area of continental Europe and Scandinavia. Not only had a much extended German state been created (*Grossdeutschland*), but direct German influence stretched from France's Atlantic shores some 2,100 kilometres eastward into the continent's interior and from the Pyrenees (dividing France from Spain) for

Fig. 5.3 Thrust to the Channel ports, May 1940

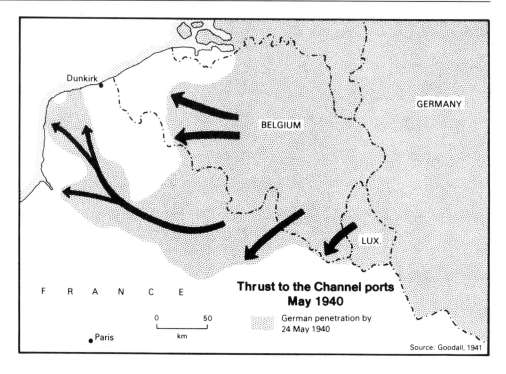

Fig. 5.4 French partition, June 1940

some 3,200 kilometres northward to beyond the Arctic Circle in occupied Norway. Here was a new German Empire won at breakneck speed. With so much of Europe under his control, Hitler and other leading Nazis saw it only as a matter of time before Britain, the one remaining belligerent, made overtures for peace. But German expectations proved fundamentally wrong. Under Winston Churchill's leadership from May 1940, the British remained intransigent against Nazi aggression. Thus Hitler moved towards a campaign to conquer Britain. By August 1940, in other words, the war was showing a logic of its own. An invasion of Britain represented a 'forward push' in

Fig. 5.5 Rumanian partition, August 1940

pursuit of a resolution of hostilities. When it had to be abandoned for reasons of logistics, including bad weather, and the inability of the *Luftwaffe* to wipe out the Royal Air Force, the focus became Russia, though not before Hitler had secured Germany's Balkan flank and made a successful thrust against British interests in North Africa.

German moves in the Balkans were precipitated in part by Russia's own territorial annexations on the eastern and southern flanks of the Reich. In June 1940, the Russians overran the three Baltic states of Estonia, Latvia and Lithuania and seized from Rumania the provinces of Northern Bukovina and Bessarabia, the latter having belonged to Russia prior to 1918. These moves reminded Hitler of the potential threat of war in the east and hence possible war on two fronts. More specifically, the Rumanian annexations threatened Germany's vital oil supplies from the Ploesti deposits. In a complicated piece of 'cloak-and-dagger' diplomacy, Hitler secured under German influence what remained of Rumanian territory (Fig. 5.5), at the same time reinforcing Hungary's place in the Nazi orbit by the transfer of Transylvania from the Rumanians. This was achieved in August 1940 and by October German troops were occupying the Ploesti oil fields.

The second factor in Hitler's Balkan adventures was the role played by Italy. Mussolini's contribution to the Axis partnership was opportunist and grossly miscalculated. Italy became formally active in the war after Hitler's successful invasion of France, capitalising on German success by securing minor territorial additions in the Alpes Maritimes. However, in October 1940, Mussolini engaged in an abortive invasion of Greece which eventually drew a British presence on Crete and on the Greek mainland. Faced with this threat, Hitler began planning for his own invasion of Greece. This was completed successfully in April 1941, having first crushed Yugoslavia when a *coup* there sabotaged plans for a peaceful accommodation with the Reich.

Fig. 5.6 The expansion of German-occupied Europe, 1939–40

Fig. 5.7 Hitler's invasion of Russia

Yugoslavia was divided up among Germany, Italy, Hungary and Bulgaria, only Croatia remaining as an autonomous (but puppet) state.

The invasion of Russia, or 'Operation Barbarossa', to give it its German code name, was launched on 22 June 1941 (Fig. 5.7). It had involved months of meticulous planning and aimed at the conquest of the entire area of European Russia, extending to the White Sea in the north and the Caucasus in the south. The sheer scale of these projected territorial acquisitions was monomaniacal. From the German border in the middle of what was originally Poland to the Volga River was roughly 1,600 kilometres. It was not much further from the same border to France's Atlantic coast. From East Prussia, the Russian capital, Moscow, was some 950 kilometres away. The length of Russia's entire European borders, from the Baltic to the Black Sea, was around 1,300 kilometres, a formidable front for any attacking or even defending army. What is more, the battle front ultimately extended to almost 2,400 kilometres as Russian territory was accumulated. The initial success of Barbarossa was startling. By mid-August, the German armies had almost reached the Dneiper River and the city of Kiev in the south, they had taken Smolensk in the centre, and they were within 160 kilometres of Leningrad in the north. In places the front had advanced 700 kilometres, and all in the space of around eight weeks. The Polish '*Blitzkrieg*' was repeated over again, helped by largely unco-ordinated Russian defence. By mid-October, the Germans had taken the greater part of the resource-rich Ukraine, including Kiev, and were poised to enter the Caucasus, they were within 160 kilometres of Moscow, and they were almost at the gates of Leningrad (Fig. 5.8). But the approaching winter of 1941/2 was to be a watershed in Hitler's land war in Europe. Steadily crippled by the appalling weather conditions of a Russian winter, the *Wehrmacht* began to encounter strong Russian resistance. The Red Army's capacity for reinforcement far exceeded German assessments and expectations. Yet more significant was the evident failure of '*Blitzkrieg*'. The entire German campaign had been developed on the assumption that Russia would be defeated by the autumn. It was manifestly not. Thus the strategy of lightning war had failed.

From the winter of 1941, Germany was forced into a war of attrition. It became a war which was to place severe strains on the German economy and ultimately to defeat it in the face of Allied resources. The Germans were to make further territorial gains in 1942, notably in the south beyond Rostov-on-Don and east to Stalingrad, but elsewhere they were pushed back from their autumn 1941 positions. The Russian recovery was slow and, as late as August 1943, the battle fronts were not much different from their positions in the autumn of 1941. Phases of counter-attacks, from both sides, were interspersed with phases of uneasy equilibrium, while the weather continued to weave its own pattern into the sequence of military engage-ments. Not until mid-summer 1944 had the Red Army reinstated its pre-war border with Poland. By this time, Hitler's western armies faced an Allied invasion in France and the feared land war on two fronts had become a reality. From mid-1943, Hitler's empire, which by then extended some 3,700 kilometres east-west from the western coast of France to the Volga River at Stalingrad, was to suffer steady erosion from nearly all quarters of the compass. By April 1945, his German state had been wiped out altogether.

Fig. 5.8 Hitler's
empire by autumn
1942

Fig. 5.8 Hitler's empire by autumn 1942

34   *Allied bombing*

Bombing raids against Germany began in May 1940 (Fig. 5.9), following Hitler's invasion of the Low Countries and of France. They continued largely uninterrupted for the ensuing five years, becoming much more intense after the United States entry into the war and after the successful D-Day landings in France in June 1944. In the single month of March 1945, British and United States planes dropped on German cities twice the bomb tonnage that fell on Britain throughout the entire war.

Allied bombing took two basic forms: precision bombing of military, industrial and transportation targets; and general 'area' bombing of industrial and urban foci (Figs 5.10 and 5.11). The former required detailed and reliable information on target locations and generally had to be carried out in daylight, in other words requiring considerable fighter support. In many ways, area bombing was a response to the difficulties of these contingencies.

Fig. 5.9 Aerial bombardment by October 1940

Aerial
bombardment
by October 1940

. Places raided by
British bombers

/// Germany and
German-occupied
territories

GREAT
BRITAIN
London

Berlin

600 mls
965 km

400 mls
643 km

200 mls
322 km

0   200
km

Source: *Serial maps*, 1940

Fig. 5.10 British bombing of German cities, 1940–45

Total civilian deaths as a result of all bombing raids were approximately 600,000, with another 800,000 injured. Over 2 million homes were destroyed and some 7.5 million people rendered homeless. These figures were exceeded only in Japan.

British
area bombing
of German cities
1940-5

Estimated percentage
of built-up area destroyed

● 67 and more

⊙ 34-66

○ 33 and less

Lübeck
Hamburg
Bremen
Stettin
Hanover
Berlin
Duisburg
Dortmund
Cologne
Bonn
Dresden
Frankfurt
Nuremberg
Stuttgart
Munich

0   200
km

Note: Includes only cities with populations of 100,000 and more in 1939
Source: Hewitt, 1983

It was blanket in coverage, it was ideally suited for night attacks, and, in the British view, was a more potent destroyer of enemy morale. Area bombing, notably of urban-industrial concentrations, became the special preserve of Britain's RAF Bomber Command.

Fig. 5.11 British area
bombing of German cities

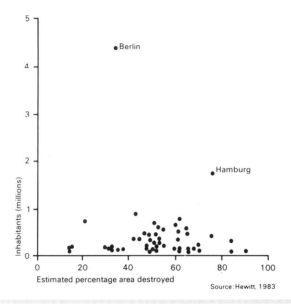

Source: Hewitt, 1983

The efficacy of these two bombing strategies is not easily established. There is no consensus, for instance, on the degree to which the German war effort was retarded. The heavy British raids on German cities from the summer of 1943 onwards have been viewed by some commentators as having served to enhance Germany's war effort by allowing War Minister Speer and others to convince Hitler and leading Nazis that a much fuller mobilisation of the economy for war was urgently needed. However, Allied bombing can be held to account for particular acute shortages in the German war economy. This was notably true of fuel oil. Attacks against synthetic oil plants at one stage brought production to a standstill (September 1944); and over the last six months of the war the German Army and the German Air Force often had more tanks and more aircraft than they had fuel to operate them. The urban-industrial concentrations of the Rhine–Ruhr area sustained some of the heaviest bombing. This reflected the great concentration of German industrial and raw material capacity in the area, but it had another, less immediately apparent significance. Much remaining industrial capacity was in some way dependent on products from the Rhine–Ruhr. The dislocation of the area was thus an indirect path to retarding the broad mass of German industry, a feature which was enhanced as precision bombing of railway lines in and around the Rhine–Ruhr gathered force, so impeding the outward flow of goods, especially coal.

35   *The Allied road to Berlin*

If, in hindsight, the German failure to take Moscow in November 1941 appears as a turning point in Hitler's European war, this was hardly the perception of the Allies, the more so given Japan's surprise attack on the US fleet at Pearl Harbor in early December of that year and the consequent extension of war to a world theatre. Events in 1942 were even less encouraging. In the summer, Germany's North African armies under Rommel drove the British east to El Alamein, within 60 miles of the Egyptian port of Alexandria, and threatened British supply routes through Suez. In the Atlantic theatre, 6.25 million tons of Allied shipping were sunk by German U-boats in 1942. By late summer, the monthly losses had reached 700,000 tons, a total that was beyond the capacity of Allied shipyards to replace. In the Far East, Japan was fast extending its empire with conquests in South-East Asia, including Burma, which posed a threat to British India. Finally, despite failure at Moscow, the German armies had penetrated the Caucasus almost to the Caspian by September.

To anyone unfamiliar with the subsequent history and outcome of the war, Hitler's empire by the late summer of 1942 would appear as the basis for a German-dominated Europe for years ahead. The resources of land and labour, the supplies of industrial raw materials and industrial plant, and the various other aggregates of economic power presented a formidable base from which to sustain it. Moreover, this was not an empire consisting of scattered territories, some of them separated by intervening seas. It was a contiguous land empire, protected by water on three of its four flanks. How, then, did this empire collapse? How was it that within three years of the German victories of mid-1942 the German state had ceased to exist?

The facts of defeat can be presented without difficulty. On the Russian Front (Fig. 5.12), Stalingrad became the pivot on which the two fighting forces advanced or retreated. Beginning in November 1942, the Russians seized the initiative and by the end of January 1943 the German forces at Stalingrad had been outmanoeuvred and had surrendered. The Caucasus was rapidly evacuated and almost the entire German Front, from the Baltic to the Black Sea, began a steady retreat. In early spring and again in early July, the Germans renewed their offensive, but with marginal success. This was followed by a Russian offensive which continued with only limited interruption into the depth of the next winter, bringing with it extensive territorial gains in the Ukraine, including Kiev. The German command made various attempts to stabilise the front here, but gains were won at tremendous loss of machines and men and rarely were they sustained. The winter of 1943/4 also saw Russian gains around Leningrad, but those in the Ukraine overshadowed all, and in February 1944 that area was again the focus of offensive. By April, Odessa had been recaptured and the Crimea cleared of Germans. Then in June and July, in a series of ferocious advances, the Germans were driven to beyond Russia's old (1939) border with Poland. Henceforward the Russian campaign split into two basic parts: the drive across northern Europe; and the operations in the Balkans. The latter made the more rapid progress. By August, the Rumanian oil-fields had been secured and Bucharest entered. Sofia fell in September and Bulgaria quickly joined in with the Red Army in the fight against the German forces, as, by then, had Rumania. Progress subsequently slowed as the Germans took strong defensive action and Hungary was not finally won until February/March 1945. The Russians then advanced on Vienna and on Prague, soon to converge with the armies of the Western Allies. Resistance on the northern front was stronger. A Russian attempt to seize Warsaw in

Fig. 5.12
Russian
counter-
attack

Russian counter-attack

Battle lines
——— 19 November 1942
- - - - 15 July 1943
— — 20 June 1944

0   250
km

Source: *Chambers Encyclopedia*, 1959

late summer 1944 failed. But Russian fortunes here were assisted by Finland's desertion of the Axis cause which pushed the Germans back to Norway. The real assault on the Polish Front came early in 1945. German defence proved locally strong but disorganised in aggregate. Berlin was soon surrounded, the city surrendering after fierce fighting early in May.

As the epic of Stalingrad unfolded in the late autumn and winter of 1942, the tide began rapidly to turn against the Germans in North Africa. In late August, Rommel attempted to drive eastward to the Nile, but the thrust proved unsuccessful. The Allies then counter-attacked in October and set in train a long rout of the German forces. Almost simultaneously, the Allies landed in Algeria and Morocco and threatened to strike a new blow to Axis

Fig. 5.13 The Normandy landings, 6 June 1944

The
**Normandy landings
6 June 1944**
Ground secured
6-13 June 1944

0   50

km

Source: Horrabin, 1946

positions from the west. Hitler responded by occupying Vichy France and flying in troops to seize French Tunisia. The North African campaign proved a relatively brief one, however. By the late spring of 1943, the Axis armies there had been defeated and North Africa became a springboard for attacks on the southern flanks of Hitler's Europe, its so-called 'soft under-belly'. The Italian and German forces were driven out of Sicily by mid-August 1943 and within weeks the Allies had landed in mainland Italy. The subsequent Italian campaign was protracted. The deposition of Mussolini and the surrender of the Italian government and its armies in September 1943 simply prompted a strong German military presence in Italy and Italian-held territory and the proclamation of a new Fascist state based in the north of the country, notionally led by Mussolini. Not until the beginning of May 1945 were the German troops in Italy forced into surrender. Italy thus became a war theatre in its own right.

The final element in the Allied campaign for the liberation of Nazi Europe came comparatively late. Ideas for an invasion of Europe from the west had been mooted early in the war, but it became a reality only in mid-summer 1944, despite persistent Russian pressure for a second European front. After months of meticulous planning and the accumulation of vast stocks of materials, a landing was successfully achieved on 6 June, D-Day (Fig. 5.13). The Allied operation was greatly assisted by the superiority of its air and naval forces. Britain provided the base for an amphibious assault on the beaches of Normandy between the mouth of the River Orne near Caen and Quineville near the base of the Cotentin peninsula. The initial task became to secure an adequate bridgehead. This was achieved by late July. Thereupon the Allied armies broke out. The United States forces thrust south towards Nantes and successfully isolated the Britanny peninsula, while British and Canadian forces engaged the Germans south of Caen. German opposition was strong and efforts were made to drive a wedge westward to

Fig. 5.14 Allied blitzkrieg in the west

the coast and so split the invading forces. However, United States forces were quickly pulled round in a southerly arc to attack the German positions south of Caen and a lightning drive was also made upon the Seine and Paris (Fig. 5.14). These moves were highly successful. The Seine was reached by mid-August and soon German forces were in rapid retreat across it. As the campaign in Normandy began to meet its objectives, a second amphibious landing was being made near Cannes in south-eastern France by United States troops. By early September, this force had reached as far north as Lyons, French forces having landed in the interim and recovered Marseilles and Toulon.

One of the Allies' most critical problems at this stage became the length of their supply lines and the need to secure ports of reinforcement further east in the English Channel. The Germans frustrated the requirement by staging last-minute holds on vital ports and in the process destroying large parts of them. However, by late September 1944, German forces had been all but expelled from French soil and the Allies were pressing forward into the Low Countries and poised to enter Germany itself. There followed a period of consolidation in which preparations were made for the final thrust into the Nazi homeland and for the crossing of the natural defensive barrier of the Rhine (Fig. 5.15). But in mid-December, Hitler ordered a counter-attack. It was made through the Ardennes along a 65-kilometre front from a base

Fig. 5.15 Allied assault on the German homelands

roughly parallel with the eastern border of Luxemburg. Within days, the German forces had penetrated some 80 kilometres. The victory was not sustained, though. Attacked by an Allied force from the south and subjected to intensive aerial bombardment, not to mention strong resistance along the front itself, the German thrust had been all but wiped out by late January 1945. Progress to the Rhine met with determined defence. The river was reached first in the south, second in the north, and, finally, by early March, in its central course extending between the Ruhr and Frankfurt-am-Main. The task of literally crossing the Rhine slowed the Allied campaign once more, but by early April its armies were moving rapidly east to the Elbe and south-east towards the Austrian and Czech borders. Co-ordinated German defence had all but disappeared. By early May, the Western Allies were nose to nose with the Red Army.

The rapid contraction of Hitler's European empire and the occupation of the German state by the Allies stands as one of the most remarkable feats of modern warfare (Fig. 5.16). Its explanation is far from simple. Numerical superiority in men and materials, together with technological advantages like radar, made a certain impact. By the late spring of 1943, for example,

Fig. 5.16 The contraction of Hitler's Europe. (left) Hitler's Europe on the eve of D-Day (6 June 1944), (right) Allied liberation to mid-February 1945

German U-boats were temporarily withdrawn from major Atlantic operations owing to disastrous losses in the face of superior Allied tracking methods. Another vital feature of German defeat was the Nazis' management of the vast array of annexed and occupied territories. A more astute conqueror would have harnessed the resources of land, materials and labour to the full, and would have played up to the grievances of the indigenous populations. None of these conditions were met or even approached. The greater part of Germany's territorial acquisitions became locked into a system which progressively alienated – in some cases liquidated – local peoples, wrought havoc with much productive activity, and installed a chaos of conflicting authority from which little that was positive could emerge. The fruits of such policies were reflected in the strength of partisan activity in occupied Russia, for example, and in the fragility of the Axis alliance as soon as the spectre of defeat became apparent. A third dimension in Germany's rapid defeat was the extreme reluctance of Hitler and Nazi Party leaders to countenance a full-scale mobilisation of resources in favour of war. This is eloquently testified in the startling fact that the peak of German armaments production was not reached until the autumn of 1944, when Hitler's empire was in full retreat and much production capacity already lost to the Allies. The failure to mobilise female labour mirrored the pattern, as did the absence throughout the war of dual shift-working in much of industry.

Finally, no explanation of German defeat can neglect the personality and will of Hitler himself. This expressed itself in most of the facets already discussed, but in others, for example the actual direction of the war, it had a most singular significance. Hitler's conception of war was a highly restricted one. It centred around '*Blitzkrieg*': administering the lightning blow, the 'smash-and-grab' technique of aggression. When campaign conditions rendered such tactics irrelevant, the '*Blitzkrieg*' mentality still remained the dominant force in the Hitler mind. To the utter dismay of many of his generals, the prevailing mould of the German war campaign after 1942 became the delivering of fatal blows to enemy forces. Counter-offensives like the one at Kursk on the Russian Front in July 1943 were accorded totally unrealistic expectations. The Ardennes offensive of December 1944 fell into the same category. Defensive or holding strategies were pursued only when force of circumstances was undeniable, where, for example, events in the field were so rapid as to render Hitler temporally out of direct control. Where events did not transpire to overtake his command, the approach became ideological rather than military. Von Paulus' Sixth Army at Stalingrad was to fight to the last man rather than surrender. To do otherwise was to undermine the Nazi view of the Germans as the *Herrenvolk*. The position of the army generals in all this was difficult and the problems intensified after Hitler assumed direct command of the army following its failure to take Moscow in the early winter of 1941. In the Normandy campaign, dissensions among the leading generals were exacerbated by Hitler's summary changes of confidence in them, dismissals being followed by reinstatements as each succeeding new command failed to stall the Allied assault.

VI Part Six

The War Machine

The outbreak of war brought no sudden fundamental changes to the Third Reich. Since 1933, Nazi Germany had existed in a state of emergency; the war merely intensified that state. For economy and society at large, the war brought home a situation which had long been prepared for: as seen, for example, in the militaristic training of the Hitler Youth, the drive for raw material self-sufficiency and, more widely, in rearmament. In the eyes of the Nazi leadership, moreover, the First World War had never been resolved to German satisfaction. As the war progressed, though, as the tactics of *'Blitzkrieg'* faltered, cracks appeared in the Third Reich's preparedness. In response, there was a steady extension in the power and jurisdiction of particular central authorities – in labour, in armaments, in raw material supply and in other sectors critical to the more rigorous conduct of the war. Yet, at the same time, often in contradiction, the authority of regional Nazi Party leaders, Gauleiters especially, was reinforced. The pattern was most acutely expressed in the eastern occupied lands where Party strongmen were quick to exploit the administrative vacuums which were presented following the turnover from military to civilian control. But the congruent state and Party administrative structures (Reichsgaue) created for Austria, western Poland and the Sudetenland in 1939/40 greatly augmented Party authority within the Greater German Reich, as did the practice of allocating the administration of contiguous western occupied zones (such as Alsace-Lorraine) to the Gauleiters of adjacent Gaue (Fig. 6.1).

At the outbreak of war, the Ministerial Council for the Defence of the Reich appointed Reich Governors and *Oberpräsidenten* as Defence Commissioners in each of the 18 military regions (*Wehrkreise*). As most of these individuals were Gauleiters, this had the appearance of enhancing Party power at an early stage. But the difficulty was that the *Wehrkreise* bore little relation either to Party regions or to the old Prussian Provinces or *Länder*. The outcome was a maze of incongruent geographical jurisdictions which severely hindered the exercise of authority (Fig. 6.2). Only in late 1942 was this chaos resolved when the Gaue themselves became the Reich Defence Zones. Henceforward, the power of Gauleiters was manifest. Indeed, as the

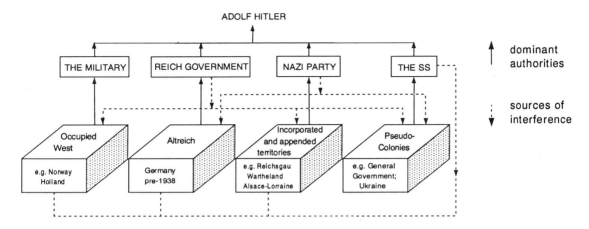

Fig. 6.1 Schematised view of dominant administrative authorities in the Third Reich, circa 1942

Fig. 6.2 The incongruent jurisdictions of military and party regions

prospect of German defeat unfolded, some Gauleiters appeared to take on the role of absolute rulers, in the mould of 'Gau-Kings'. More and more they came to epitomise the operation of the *Führerprinzip* as Hitler's delegate territorial leaders.

Even before the war, Hitler's participation in the day-to-day affairs of government had been steadily diminishing. With the outbreak of war, he effectively ceased to be Reich Chancellor, the task being delegated to the Cabinet Council for the Defence of the Reich, chaired by Goering. In practice, this body never operated as a council. Decrees were issued under the Council's authority, but these primarily came from Goering or Frick and did not require agreement of the full council, merely counter-signatures of certain members. The outcome was inevitably to promote independence among Reich Ministries and hence to encourage rivalries. These problems were compounded by the fact that decrees did not extend automatically to cover the eastern zones of occupation or the various civilian and military administrations which obtained in the occupied west. This, in turn, was part of a wider problem of the increasing administrative disunity of the Third Reich: as between the *Altreich* of pre-1938, the incorporated territories like Danzig-West Prussia and Wartheland in which Party and state administrations were fused (the so-called 'model Gaue'), appended territories such as Luxembourg or the Polish Government-General, and the pseudo-colonies of the East in what was formerly Russia (see Fig. 6.1 above). All displayed variant administrative forms which bred confusion and conflict; what is more, the situation became a self-polarising one. The supreme irrationality of Nazi administration, though, was perhaps to be found in the survival of the Gau units to the very end and in the enhanced functions ascribed to them from late 1942. Modelled largely on the Reichstag electoral districts, they were already anachronisms by the mid-1930s. They survived to the end because the essence of National Socialist power lay in personalities, not bureaucracies, in Gauleiters not Gaue.

37   *The army*

The Army had long been a key power block in Germany. It remained so under the Nazi regime, but over time came more and more under Hitler's influence and direct control. The pattern showed first in 1938 with the formation of the OKW (*Oberkommando de Wehrmacht* or Armed Forces High Command) of which Hitler made himself chief (Fig. 6.3). It was dramatically extended when, with the first reverses of the Russian campaign in late 1941, Hitler also appointed himself Army Commander. Thereafter, the story became one of persistent interference and change in the army's command organisation and tactics. From the German side, the land war was played out almost entirely according to the *Führer*'s will. The German army's inability to stem the Allied invasion of France, the débâcle in the Ardennes in 1944/5 and the various battle failures in the east were all tied in some measure to Hitler's own prosecution of the war. And the diminishing authority of army leaders is no better demonstrated than in the Stauffenberg bomb plot of July 1944: the most determined assassination attempt (and the nearest to being successful) emanated from within army ranks. The turnover of leading army personnel during the whole course of the war was formidable. Only one out of 18 field marshals survived to keep his position; no less than 10 were relieved of their commands and sent home. Likewise, out of 36 full generals, only three survived in post; the number relieved totalled 18.

Neither the navy nor the air force enjoyed the position of importance occupied by the army; either before or during the course of the war. In terms

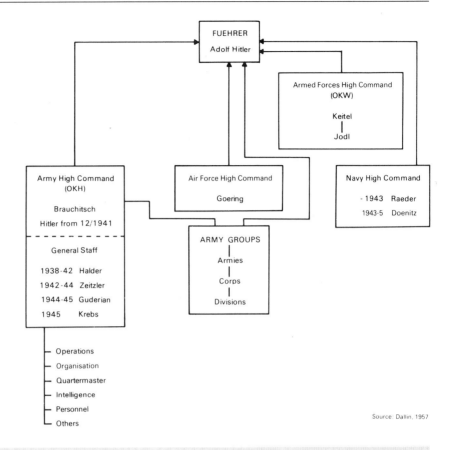

Fig. 6.3 The High Command (Army)

Note: the OKW was supposed to co-ordinate the policy of all three services, but failed to do so in practice

Source: Dallin, 1957

of simple manpower, the army upon mobilisation in September 1939 had some 3.7 million troops; air force personnel numbered 400,000 and navy personnel just 50,000. This is not an entirely adequate perspective, though, because both the air force and the navy, by their nature, had far higher ratios of capital to men. Aircraft production as an individual armaments sector, for example, consistently absorbed the highest percentage of spending alongside other primary armaments sectors like tanks and munitions. Over 1942 to 1944, the figure averaged around 40 per cent. On the wider question of the prosecution of the war, however, it remains true that the army formed by far the dominant element. By 1942, for instance, the bulk of the German surface fleet had been effectively immobilised. The Atlantic U-boat packs, while enormously successful up to the summer of 1942, were soon blunted by Allied tracking, which resulted in their temporary withdrawal for several months in mid-1943. The air force fared somewhat better and, of course, fulfilled a significant adjunct role relative to army operations. But from mid-way through the war, its capacity was increasingly inadequate relative to the demands placed upon it; this was especially true in fighter defence against the Allied bombing campaign in the last years of the war. Thus it was the army which shouldered the burden of attack and defence, the latter especially. And it was relatively easier to reinforce, replace and re-equip the army than either of the other services.

The German army also had an importance beyond its intrinsic utilitarian role. The power and traditions of the Prussian officer corps require little rehearsing here, save the necessity to underline Hitler's growing domination of the army leadership from 1938. But beyond this lay the relationship between *Wehrmacht* and the Nazi *Weltanschauung*. Until preparations for the invasion of Russia, the military remained clearly separated from Nazi political ideology. But as the Russian war plans and the war itself unfolded in 1941, Hitler sought a fusion of ideological and military warfare. By and large he was successful. The majority of army leaders joined in the war of extermination against 'Jewish Bolshevism' and 'Asiatic Barbarism', sometimes seeking their own specific justifications for doing so. This is not to say that the appalling conditions of the Russian Front, the long-standing antagonism of German and Slav, and the intensity of Russian partisan activity were insignificant contributors to the inhuman sufferings of Russians, soldiers and civilians alike, at the hands of the German army. Furthermore, the activities of the SS and its *Einsatzgruppen*, by comparison, were doubly savage. It is nevertheless true that the German army in Russia fulfilled a task which its western counterpart hardly even addressed and that international codes of military conduct vanished on the Russian front as Hitler's infamous order to the army to liquidate all Russian political leaders and Commissars was carried out.

In the seven years of Nazi rule up to the end of 1939, the German army had increased in size roughly 18 times over. Such a rapid rate of growth had produced inevitable problems in achieving a sufficient officer corps not to mention the wider question of equipment. The age structure of the army upon mobilisation for war was also somewhat unsatisfactory. There were many veterans from the First World War, including officers. The reason was that the various industries associated with rearmament had absorbed men from the lower age cohorts who could not be removed without damaging effects; such skilled workers were not readily replaced. These different problems were far from resolved as the war unfolded (Fig. 6.4). The concept

Fig. 6.4 Armed forces manpower in relation to total German manpower, 1939–45

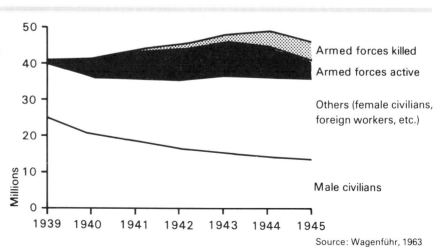

Source: Wagenführ, 1963

Fig. 6.5 The Kdf foreign organisation, 1942

The vast scale of the armed forces commitment on the Russian front is reflected in the provisions of the German Labour Front (DAF) through its *Kraft durch Freude* organisation. *Kraft durch Freude* homes acted as convalescent centres for injured soldiers.

The Kdf foreign organisation
1942

■ KdF homes

▣ Ditto under construction

• Berlin
• Kursk
• Kiev

0   500
km

Source: Dienst-gemeinschaft Kraft durch Freude im Kriegsjahr, 1942, BA Koblenz

of '*Blitzkrieg*' and the remarkably short duration of the offensives against Poland, the Low Countries and France offered obvious mitigation. However, the manpower and the equipment needs for the attack on Russia were formidable, even allowing for a short war (Fig. 6.5). The German Field Army in September 1939 numbered 2.76 million; by June 1941 it was 3.8 million and, of these, 3.3 million were deployed in Barbarossa. Henceforward, the needs of protracted land warfare on several fronts, coupled with increasing levels of attrition, soon magnified the army's problems, often beyond anything previously encountered. The attrition is reflected in the relatively slower growth of the field army alongside the multiplying theatres of war. A year after the launch of Barbarossa, for instance, it was only 3.95 million. By the summer of 1943, it was only 4.48 million.

Hitler's relations with the army over this later period became increasingly strained and were in part responsible for the mushroom expansion of the *Waffen-SS*. At the opening of the Russian campaign, it incorporated around 165,000 men. By April 1945, some 800,000 men had served in SS ranks and 40 SS divisions had been raised. Moreover, Hitler had also authorised the formation of an SS Army Corps. Previously, SS divisions had always been distributed singly throughout the army. SS divisions acquired reputations as formidable fighting forces, but this was not true generally, particularly of the much enlarged *Waffen-SS* after 1942 with its increasingly lower percentage of German nationals. For Himmler, the enlarged *Waffen-SS* offered an insurance towards SS domination in the Nazis' post-war European order. The 'watering down' of its elite quality was worrying but not without potential reward.

Perhaps one of the most striking features of the German Army during the Second World War was the infantry's reliance on horse transport. The pervasive image of the German military is one of superior mobility, of motorisation. This perception is encapsulated in the Polish '*Blitzkrieg*' of 1939: the triumph of machine over muscle. And yet nearly twice as many horses were utilised by the German army in 1939–45 as in 1914–18 (2.7 million against 1.4 million). By the winter of 1943/4, only 16 per cent of German divisions were fully motorised. The consequences were critical in the kind of mobile war which was fought with the Russians in the east.

The success of Albert Speer in achieving a quantum leap in armaments production after 1942 must naturally be set alongside the inadequacies of mobility. By 1944, the monthly tonnage of armoured vehicles (tanks, assault guns etc.) was roughly 15 times what it had been in 1940. However, against the forces asembled by Stalin, such an achievement does not look so impressive. In the great Russian frontal attack on Army Group Centre in mid-summer 1944, for example, the Soviets assembled nearly 200 divisions with 2.5 million men, 6,000 tanks and assault guns, 45,000 guns and mortars and 7,000 aircraft. German production of tanks, assault guns and similar armoured vehicles was but 1,500 a month. This had to service the demands of western and southern as well as eastern war theatres. The Germans also faced increasing quality hazards in their armament supplies, the consequence of the conscription of foreign labour in the armaments industries, including prisoners of war. Of equivalent note were the dramatic weapon failures, for instance the giant Ferdinand tank first deployed in the Battle of Kursk in 1943. Even so, the technical superiority of some German weaponry was freely acknowledged by Allied forces right up to the closing months of the war.

38 *The SS*

The wartime years were ones of determined fulfilment for the SS. As the Reich's eastern borders were extended deeper into Europe towards Asia, there was opened up a massive trial ground in which the racial and ideological schemes of the SS could be tested and refined. The Third Reich's transition to war from 1938 was a watershed for the SS in that it changed from being primarily a support for the Nazi regime and a special Führer executive to being also an organisation pursuing its own goals and particular conceptions of future German nationhood under Himmler's direction. There was, however, a dimension to the wartime SS which undermined the singularity of its purpose and the force of its authority. The SS grew enormously in size as the war progressed. In June 1944, it had reached 800,000 men. By that time, some 100,000 had already perished in war

Note: See text and glossary for terms

Source: Dallin, 1957

Fig. 6.6 The SS organisation (simplified)

action. By the close of the war, up to 300,000 SS men were to have lost their lives. The bulk of wartime SS men were soldiers, in fact, serving in the *Waffen-SS* or the *Wehrmacht*. For the majority of them, the ideological and racial struggles in occupied lands were second-hand knowledge, activities in which they played little direct part. These tasks were performed by a tiny fraction of the SS, perhaps no more than 10,000 men, including officers. Even within this grouping, there were SS men whose commitment fell some way short of the all-embracing views of Himmler and his closest SS officers. The war, in other words, saw a progressive watering down of the SS as the 'gene-pool' of a new Germany, as the vanguard of a superior Nordic/Aryan culture destined to dominate Europe and Eurasia. The vast eastern conquests may have afforded unprecedented proving grounds for the SS, but the hard core of true believers did not grow in tandem, indeed could not, given the manpower needs of war with Russia.

A vital facet of the SS from the late 1930s was the scale of its bureaucracy (Fig. 6.6). The 'state within a state' syndrome is an understandable one, if not entirely appropriate. The central organ of this bureaucracy was the RSHA (*Reichssicherheitshauptamt* – Reich Security Office). Its title gave the impression of a formal state organisation. In fact, it was an SS agency and represented the outcome of years of creeping infiltration by the SS apparatus into the various police organisations of the state. Himmler's installation in 1936 as Chief of German Police, alongside his position as SS Chief, had set the process firmly in train. By the beginning of the war, it was only the regional and local police administrations, involving the general Order Police, which remained outside direct SS control. Otherwise, the RSHA incorporated the Gestapo, KRIPO (*Kriminalpolizei* – Criminal Police) and the intelligence organisations, along with the SD (*Sicherheitsdienst* – Security Service) built up for the SS by Heydrich. As war progressed, moreover, RSHA jurisdiction was extended to include departments such as that which oversaw occupation policies. But the significance of this giant central police apparatus went beyond the business of police activity *per se* and the safeguarding of the Nazi state. It was also aimed at moulding the new National Socialist order in a post-war Europe. In this sense, the police organisation became a political agency in itself.

Several of the remaining central offices of the SS bureaucracy reflected these longer-term goals. This was notably true of the RKFDV (*Reichskommissariat für die Festigung deutschen Volkstums* – Reich Commission for the Strengthening of German Nationhood) established in 1939, with the SS Chief as its first commissar. Himmler was charged with the task of resettling ethnic Germans within the Reich's borders and of weeding out ethnic groups which were considered undesirable. Beyond such SS main offices as that dealing with the recruiting and organisation of manpower, the other primary part of the SS bureaucracy was the WVHA (*Wirtschafts und Verwaltungshauptamt* – the chief SS Economic and Administrative office) which held the task of running the concentration and labour camps and of operating the growing range of SS economic enterprises.

The concentration camp system underwent a phenomenal expansion over the course of the war. Whereas the camps had started life mainly as internment centres for political undesirables and opponents of the Nazi regime, from the late 1930s they became places for detaining *social* undesirables like vagrants, thieves, homosexuals, scaremongers, unco-operative nationals from seized or occupied territories, and, above all, *racial* undesirables ranging from gypsies to Jews. The camps grew because they became sumps for the 'cleansing' of European society according to Nazi racial dogma and because Hitler's successive conquests progressively enlarged the area in which this operation could take place. As the war unfolded, moreover, the camps increasingly became institutions for forced labour, servicing both the general demands of the war economy and the more specific requirements of the SS economic administration.

By 1943/4, there were 23 major concentration camps extending from the Low Countries and eastern France to the former Baltic states and eastern Poland (Fig. 6.7). But added to these was a vast array of affiliated camps, perhaps numbering as many as 1,000 by 1943/4 (Figs 6.8 and 6.9). Although the chronically inhuman conditions of detention were broadly similar across the range of camps – chances of survival were rarely much more than 30 per cent – some camps had special tasks. The most infamous of these was the extermination of the Jewish race, which fell to the camps in the east: namely Auschwitz, Chelmno, Treblinka, Sobibor, Lublin and Belzec. Statistics about concentration camp detainees are few. Figures of the number of living inmates (in January 1945 there were some 714,000) are comparatively meaningless. To be alive in a concentration camp was exceptional. Millions perished or were murdered, unrecorded.

The extermination policies inevitably conflicted in some degree with the desire to use concentration camp labour in SS enterprises and with the more

Fig. 6.7
The chief
concen-
tration
camps

**The chief
concentration camps**

—·—·— Greater Germany

— — — Russian front

0   500
km

1	Vairara	7	Lublin	13	Mauthausen	19	Flossenbürg
2	Klooga	8	Krakau	14	Neuengamme	20	Niederhagen
3	Riga	9	Auschwitz (3 camps)	15	Bergen-Belsen	21	Dachau
4	Kaven	10	Gross-Rosen	16	Arbeitsdorf	22	Herzogenbusch
5	Sutthof	11	Ravensbrück	17	Mittelbau	23	Natzweiler
6	Warsaw	12	Sachsenhausen	18	Buchenwald		

Source: Hilgemann, 1984

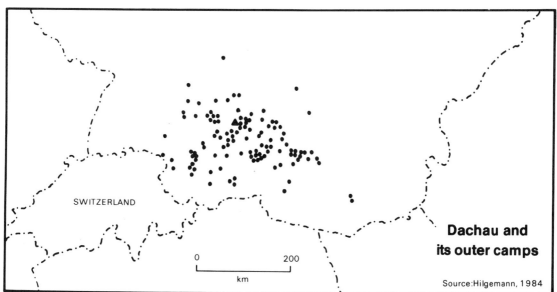

SWITZERLAND

0   200
km

**Dachau and
its outer camps**

Source: Hilgemann, 1984

Fig. 6.8 Dachau and its outer camps

Fig. 6.9 Principal
nationalities at Dachau
concentration camp at the
time of liberation

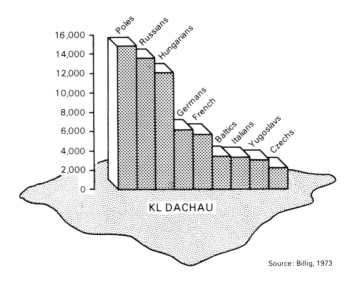

Source: Billig, 1973

Fig. 6.10 Primary SS
enterprises, Spring 1944

general demand for labour in the increasingly strained German war
economy. As long as new detainees continued to arrive at roughly
replacement rates or better, the dual purposes could be realised. When
numbers declined, or when labour demands rose, conflicts with the
Armaments Ministry and among the various arms of the SS bureaucracy
became inevitable. The connection between the SS manufacturing enterprises
and camp labour is reflected in their geographical coincidence (Fig. 6.10). In
1943, the earth and stone-working division (DEST – *Deutsche Erd und
Steinwerke Gmbh*) of the SS Economic and Administrative office had an

Fig. 6.11 SS organisation for Greater Germany, 1941

SS organisation for
Greater Germany 1941

— · — Greater Germany

— — — 1937 German borders

———— SS regions (as military
regions/Wehrkreise)

• Sites of divisions 81 -
125 of General SS

Source: Koehl, 1983

annual turnover of 14.8 million Reichsmarks. The armaments division (DAW – *Deutsche Ausrüstugswerke Gmbh*) had a turnover of 23 million RM in the same year. Before the war much SS economic activity was orientated towards craft enterprise or semi-luxury goods. The emphasis changed from 1939 with the armaments sector recording the most rapid expansion. In the last years of the war, the SS Economic and Administrative office began hiring out concentration camp labour for use in state-run enterprises and in private industry. Such hirings brought significant profits to the SS, although these sometimes accrued not to the organisation itself but to leading SS officers. The average daily hire charge was 4 to 6 Reichsmarks. In the last year of the war, up to 500,000 camp inmates toiled in this way, perhaps half of them for industrial giants like Krupps and IG-Farben.

General conclusions about the SS are not made with ease. It was an organisation which grew and changed incessantly, often inconsistently, and the exigencies of war wove their own complicating thread (Fig. 6.11). In many ways the SS was a microcosm of the Third Reich itself. It became beset by the same kinds of overlapping and conflicting administrative jurisdictions. Its leading personnel were persistent opportunists, as were so many of Hitler's leaders, Himmler among them. The energy and dynamism generated within the Third Reich were replicated within the SS; the vast concentration camp system was alone testament enough to this. But the very elements which contributed to the momentum and force of the SS eventually proved its undoing. The system did not admit of consolidation. Power became too readily diffused and too idiosyncratic in exercise. The SS had no Speer to instil some semblance of central direction. Whereas the Reich was in some measure galvanised by the onset of total war, the SS was increasingly divided by it. The political and ideological goals became entangled with the opportunities for profits in servicing the war economy; with the increasing secularisation of the massive *Waffen-SS* as military reverse after military reverse made the war a patriotic rather than an ideological one; and with the complex manoeuvrings for retrenchment and survival as the domains of the SS in occupied Europe shrank and it was forced into open competition with the economic and military machines.

39   *Policies of occupation*

The extension of Hitler's Germany deep into Eurasia, as well as the conquest of Western Europe and much of Scandinavia, posed immediate problems of administration. Once military victory had been secured and the military position stabilised in strategic terms, the question arose as to the nature of subsequent German control and organisation. The pattern that emerged was a complex one (Figs 6.12, 6.14 and 6.16). It reflected needs of economic exploitation, the hunger for power among leading Nazi Party figures, the differing measures of civilian co-operation in occupied territories, and the ideological and racial ideals for a Nazi-dominated post-war Europe. As the war ran its course, moreover, policies of occupation evolved corre- spondingly. Increased civilian resistance and partisan activity, growing pressures for

Fig. 6.12 Occupied territories in Central Europe

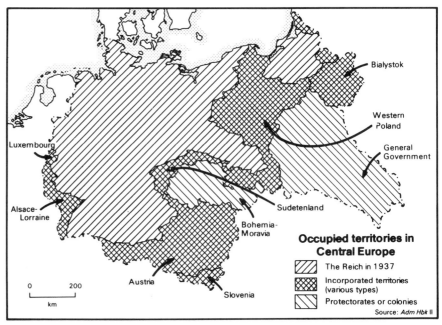

Occupied territories in Central Europe

Bialystok

Western Poland

Luxembourg

General Government

Alsace-Lorraine

Sudetenland

Bohemia-Moravia

Occupied territories in Central Europe

Austria

Slovenia

▨	The Reich in 1937
▩	Incorporated territories (various types)
▨	Protectorates or colonies

Source: *Adm Hbk* II

0   200
km

Fig. 6.13 Planned system of market and central towns in a part of Reichsgau Wartheland

Although Wartheland enjoyed an existence of less than five years, and in all that time Germany was at war, this did not prevent schemes for territorial re-organisation and changes in the urban system.

greater industrial production, Allied bombing raids and military reverses on land all combined to intensify the force of occupation policies. Labour was conscripted on an increasing scale for work in Greater Germany, the whole of occupied Europe was combed for Jews, SS policies of extermination were carried to their final conclusion, while police and SS terror broke new bounds of ferocity. In hindsight, the pattern of Nazi occupation organisation was haphazard and inefficient. But this was a predictable outcome given the conflicting power blocks which characterised the *Hitler state*. It also reflected the simple fact that trained administrative personnel were in short supply. Not only were Hitler's plans for his new German Empire ill-formed and transitory, but so was the machinery for managing it.

In very broad terms, policies of occupation followed one of three models. In Norway, Denmark, Belgium, Holland and France, German control consisted mainly of installing a military or civilian commissioner to oversee what were otherwise relatively unchanged national administrations. Within this, there was considerable requisitioning of industrial capacity, but national and cultural identities did not become targets for Nazi Germanisation.

A second category of Nazi occupation policy involved incorporation into the German state, to form Greater Germany (Fig. 6.12). Austria was the first of these incorporated territories. Subsequently, they extended to include the Czech Sudetenland, Memel, Danzig, Eupen-Malmedy, extensive parts of Western Poland, Luxemburg, Alsace-Lorraine, Slovenia and Bialystok. Some of these lands were formally incorporated under Reich law; others were incorporated on a *de facto* basis. Alsace and Lorraine, for instance, were administered by the Gauleiters of adjacent Gaue. Incorporation into Germany naturally carried with it certain penalties for the peoples and cultures involved. The consequences were greatest in the Polish areas, where native

Fig. 6.14
The administration of occupied Russia

The administration of
occupied Russia

⊖ ⊖   Front line, autumn 1942
– – –   Administrative areas
– · —   International borders

REICHSKOMMISSARIAT
OSTLAND

GREATER
GERMANY

BIALYSTOK

•Moscow

MILITARY
AREA

GENERAL
GOVERNMENT

REICHSKOMMISSARIAT
UKRAINE

HUNGARY

RUMANIA

0   200
km

Source: Hilberg, 1961

Poles were forcibly uprooted to make way for ethnic Germans from the Baltic states and south-east Europe. Wholesale Germanisation became the pattern, often with scant regard for humanitarian considerations. From the dismantled Polish state, Danzig-West Prussia and Wartheland became formally constituted *Reichsgaue*, administrative units in which state and Party jurisdictions were coincident (Fig. 6.13). Change was least in those territories which already had extensive German populations; here persecution and terror were little different from that already found within Germany itself.

The third group of occupied territories formed what were ostensibly colonies. They consisted of the remnants of Poland and Czechoslovakia and, above all, vast tracts of conquered Russian territory (Figs 6.12, 6.14 and

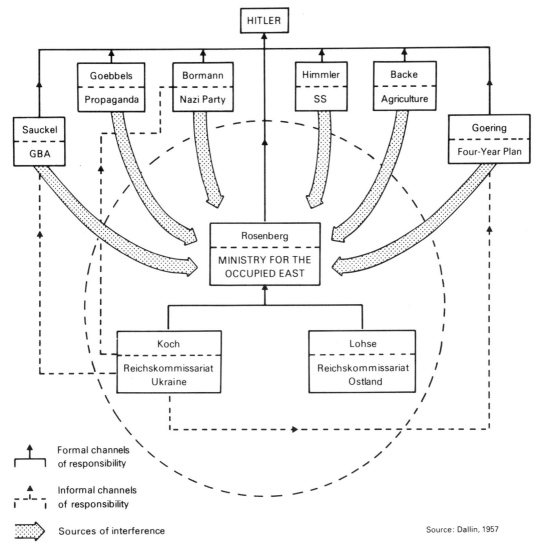

Fig. 6.15 The chaotic Nazi bureaucracy in occupied Russia

Even Goebbels was led to describe Rosenberg's charge as the 'Ministry of Chaos'

6.16). This was to be the great land empire in the east of which Hitler so often talked: the 'bread-basket' of the thousand-year Reich in which ethnic Germans and other pure-bred Nordic groups would be settled in fulfilment of Nazi ideals for a new-born peasantry. The ruthless corollary was enslavement and displacement of the indigenous peoples, the destruction of their society and the immediate liquidation of its political elites and Jewish populations. It was in Russia in particular that the full force of this Nazi ideology was felt. Special Gestapo and SS commandos (*Einsatzgruppen*) followed in the wake of victorious army units to purge the conquered areas of Bolsheviks and other enemies of the Nazi state. On Hitler's express orders, all political leaders and commissars in Russia were to be summarily executed. The Jews in these Russian territories suffered a similar fate. Some

Fig. 6.16 The planned German empire in Russia

2.25 million perished, either massacred by the *Einsatzgruppen* or deported to concentration and extermination camps.

To a growing degree, the *Einsatzgruppen* emerged as upholders of political security in the eastern territories and as an authority which overrode that of the military. Thus was formed the basis for SS domination in the East. The military was not fully acquiescent in this role. In Poland as well as in Russia, it relinquished the 'normal' administrative role of a victorious army and thereby paved the way for SS rule. But in Russia, in particular, all kinds of conflicts arose over who had authority in the rear of the battle areas, a position which became compounded as the front line was forced into retreat (Fig. 6.14). The military's somewhat tangential role in eastern occupation policy contrasted with its largely undisputed dominance in the western occupied areas.

The structure of administration for Hitler's eastern conquests never proceeded far beyond temporary expedient (Figs 6.15 and 6.16). In Russia, there were created the *Reichskommissariats* Ostland and Ukraine, headed by prominent Gauleiters. Erich Koch (East Prussia) took control of the Ukraine, while the Ostland went to Lohse, Gauleiter of Schleswig-Holstein. The Nazi

Fig. 6.17 The planned autobahn system for central Europe

This map was published by *Reichsautobahnen Direktion* as early as December 1941. For purposes of autobahn planning, the Polish Government-General was included as part of Germany. The planned network also extended into Belgium and Holland. Much of the plan was a pipe-dream: the resources were never available to realise it.

'philosopher', Alfred Rosenberg, became Reich Minister for the Occupied Territories in the east, thereby laying claim for state as compared to Party control. Hitler's original scheme for Russia envisaged a total of four *Reichskommissariats*, taking in Muscovy and the Caucasus, but these last two never materialised. In the *Reichskommissariat* Ostland, there was some use of native personnel in the civil administration formed by the Germans. But in the Ukraine, German personnel carried out the task alone.

In the rump Czechoslovak state, labelled by the Germans the Protectorate of Bohemia-Moravia (see Fig. 6.12 above), a rather greater degree of native autonomy was allowed. The Germans installed a Reich Protector, but permitted a series of Czech departments of government. Even so, German control of political power and security limited the extent to which Czech wishes were carried out. What remained of the Polish state was translated by the Germans into the Government-General (see again Fig. 6.12 above). This territory enjoyed a much lesser degree of autonomy than Bohemia-Moravia. Some Poles were employed in the lower ranks of administration, but the entire machinery of government was otherwise German, as were its principal personnel. Far more than the Czechs, the Poles were viewed as an inferior, subject race. And the Government-General, although initially the focus of economic exploitation, soon followed the fate of the rest of Poland under a campaign of racial and cultural repression, spearheaded by the SS. The highly improvised nature of Hitler's plans for the government and administration of the east played readily into the hands of the Party Gauleiters and Himmler's SS. Ultimately, though, it was the various offices of the SS machine, which more often then not exercised the primary authority, notwithstanding the deep internal rivalries.

40 *Armaments*

The realities of German armaments production over the five and a half years of war were not fully appreciated until several decades after the war's end. And even today, grey areas remain as a result of deficiencies in the historical record. The almost universal perception of the western powers was that Germany was re-arming 'in depth' from the very early years of the National Socialist regime. This view persisted through the first years of the war and was not properly confounded even when the scale of armaments production advanced rapidly from 1942 onwards, reaching its peak only in July 1944 (Fig. 6.18), by which time many of Hitler's European conquests (and hence additional resource bases) had been lost to the Allied advance. The mistake reflected a basic inability to comprehend the '*Blitzkrieg*' style of warfare which Hitler employed with such success between September 1939 and late 1941 (Fig. 6.19). The public rhetoric of Nazi leaders and the warlike activities of organisations like the Hitler Youth may have sounded otherwise, but the accompanying diagrams reveal very clearly that, in armaments, Germany was far removed from total war when seen alongside the other combatant powers and against the performance it registered between 1942 and 1944.

The remarkable success and speed of Hitler's early campaigns and the fact that Germany alone set the nature and pace of events in the first years of war combined to enhance the strategy of '*Blitzkrieg*', whatever its underlying tactical and economic advantages (Fig. 6.20). The attempts to shift armament priorities between the army, navy and air force in accordance with Hitler's

Source: Noakes and Pridham, 1974

Source: Wagenführ, 1963

Fig. 6.18 (left) Rates of armaments production of combatant powers (1940=100)
Fig. 6.19 (right) Proportion of German industrial production devoted to war materials (at 1943 prices)

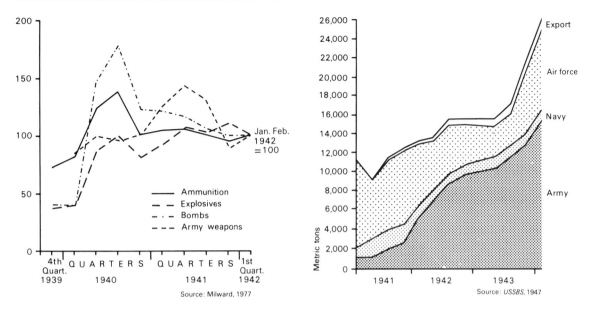

Fig. 6.20 (left) Indices of production of selected armaments in Germany, 1939–41 (average monthly indices)

Fig. 6.21 (right) TNT allocations (monthly averages for quarter year)

planned offensives were viable so long as the initiative remained in German hands (Fig. 6.21). The weakness of '*Blitzkrieg*', especially as it operated in the Third Reich, was that it contained little margin for expansion. Counter-initiatives which accorded ill with Hitler's campaign plans or German offensives which lost their momentum proved its undoing. A few of the danger signs were apparent in the Battle of Britain and in the subsequent preparations for a seaborne invasion of Britain. But they assumed real significance in the early autumn of 1941 as the Russian campaign faltered and, later, as the Soviet Armies began their own attacks. '*Blitzkrieg*' might have been less readily confounded if there had been a more rigorous and efficient system for managing it. But in true National Socialist mould, it was prey to the competitive struggles of the different service chiefs and to *ad hoc* methods of arms procurement, both within and between the service sectors.

The transfer from '*Blitzkrieg*' to armament in depth was not a rapid one, for it required a far greater measure of central direction and control than existed up to the autumn of 1941. It also needed the understanding and co-operation of the population and the Party. Moves in the former direction had begun early in 1940 when Fritz Todt was appointed to resolve a crisis over copper supplies. Success in this task led to his appointment as Minister for Armaments and Munitions in March 1940 and to the progressive rationalisation of armaments production, planning and research which was to bear such fruit under the later direction of Albert Speer, the man who took over the Ministry following Todt's untimely death in a plane crash early in 1942.

The central feature of German armaments administration in the second half of the war was the system of committee organisation. This acted to co-ordinate the armaments demands of the three services, to rationalise those

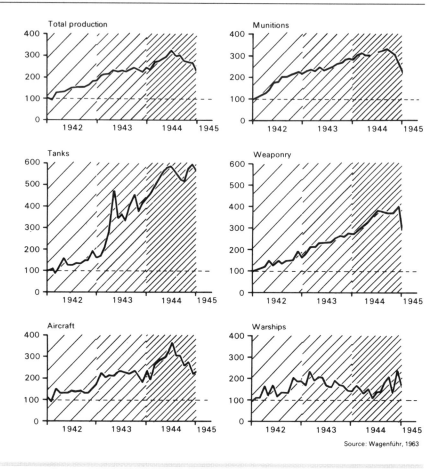

Fig. 6.22 Indices of armaments production in Germany (January–February 1942 = 100)

Source: Wagenführ, 1963

demands in relation to the factors of supply and to achieve a more efficient functional and geographical organisation of arms production and development. Albert Speer thus came to preside over an administrative regime which, with the progressive addition of wider controls like those over general raw material allocation and planning, became the central force in the German war economy, eclipsing Goering's Four-Year-Plan Organisation in much the same way as that office had earlier superseded various functions of the Economics Ministry. The OKW's (*Oberkommando der Wehrmacht* – Armed Forces High Command) War Economy and Armaments Office met a rather similar fate with the rise of Speer's Ministry.

The singular facet of this great armaments expansion was its reliance on private industry. Speer's ministerial empire operated primarily as a guiding force in a production project which handed the basic tasks of armament manufacture, research and development to factory managers and industrialists. The spectacular feats of armaments production from 1942 onwards would have been impossible without the agency of private enterprise. Speer's scheme can be described as the mobilisation of self-interest and the armaments industries tell their own story (Fig. 6.22). Over 1943 to 1944, German armaments production increased roughly threefold at a time when Allied bombing was gathering steadily in

Fig. 6.23 German explosive plants

Unlike so much basic industry, the German explosive industry was a relatively well-dispersed one. Moreover, the locational pattern of new plants established during the course of the war reinforced this. The aggregate growth in capacity between December 1939 and September 1944 was approximately four-fold.

momentum. Tank production registered the most remarkable advances, notably after winter 1942, as the war against Russia became one of attrition.

In some ways, the Speer Ministry represents an aberrant organisational form in Hitler's Germany in that its executive structure was relatively unambiguous. The conflicting and overlapping competencies that characterised so many institutions of the *Hitler state* were much less evident, a reflection of Speer's political skills, his confident relations with Hitler, and the harsh requirements of defensive war on two fronts. But the passage was not uniformly easy. In the management of labour for the armaments sector, Speer had to bow to the will of the General Plenipotentiary for Labour appointed by Hitler in spring 1942. Similarly, Speer and his committee system regularly met opposition from Party officials, the Gauleiters especially, over requirements to cut raw material allocations for consumer goods production and over the need for transfers of industrial plant in order to achieve a more rational spatial organisation of arms production. There were also persistent battles with the SS, as in the case of control of the great Skoda armaments works in Czechoslovakia. Hence political limitations remained to deflect the goals of the centre-piece of the German war machine. And parallel limitations sprang from the priority Hitler demanded for his secret weapons programme.

The V-bombs

The course of wars has in varying measure been affected by the development of novel forms of weaponry. The successful development and use of the atomic bomb by the Americans was decisive in forcing the Japanese surrender in August 1945. In Germany, the last years of the war saw much expenditure and research effort on the development and production of the V-1 and V-2 bombs, weapons intended for long-range bombardment (Fig. 6.24). The V-1 was a pilotless, jet-propelled aircraft which was launched from specially constructed ramps. It had a maximum flying time of about one hour, whereupon it literally fell to the ground with its warhead. The V-2 was a rocket which used liquid oxygen and alcohol as its fuel. This gave rise to a gas velocity nearly twice that obtained from the combustion of gunpowder and meant that, after 60 seconds' flight, the rocket had reached a height of 22 to 23 miles. By this time the fuel had been expended and the rocket fell in a relatively uncontrolled fashion, though approximating a parabolic path. It could carry a warhead of up to a ton in weight.

The first of the V-1 weapons was launched shortly after the Normandy landings in June 1944 and was directed at London. Subsequently, both weapons were used against London and also against the port of Antwerp. Their impact on the final course of the war and also on Germany's fortunes

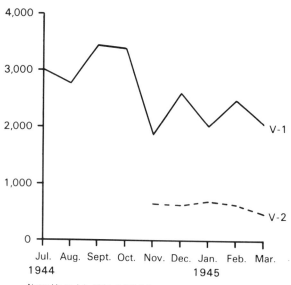

Fig. 6.24 Production of V-1 and V-2 weapons, July 1944 – March 1945

Note: Up to July 1944, 1,979 V-1 weapons produced; 345 V-2

Source: Wagenführ, 1963

was negligible, though. Despite sustained production to the very last months, the weapons lacked accuracy and reliability. An even more critical handicap was the location of many launching sites on the Channel coast beyond Germany's borders; later in 1944, these steadily fell into Allied hands. The Nazi propaganda machine, however, cast the weapons as likely to change the course of the war. Taking its cue from Hitler, who had referred to a battery of secret weapons late in 1942 and who was to maintain a blind faith in their strategic power to the end, Goebbels' Propaganda Ministry made them a continuous focus of faith against defeat not only to the mass of the people, but to soldiers and military leaders.

41   *The supply of materials*

Long before the war, the National Socialist leadership had been conscious of the uncertain supply of a variety of materials, agricultural as well as industrial. In both sectors, policies had been enacted to ameliorate these weaknesses and also to replace imports with increased domestic output, particularly those imports originating from countries thought likely to be unreliable with the prospect of war. The success of these measures was highly variable between sectors. Moreover, the territorial annexations and conquests from 1938 onwards to some extent undercut their purpose. The industrial and raw material capacities of a long line of European states soon became at Nazi Germany's disposal. And states which threw in their lot with Germany added to the total. Rumania dominated the latter group with its large mineral oil output, most of which became available to the German cause.

With so large an area of Europe under German control or influence, one might have supposed that problems of material supply would have become a feature of the past, especially given the Nazis' callous attitudes to indigenous populations and economies in some of the occupied lands. This was not true, however. The reasons were basically twofold. The transition from 1942 towards an economy much more fully geared to war and to armament 'in depth' placed greatly enhanced demands on material supply and began to expose critical weak links. But it was not simply a problem of resource bottlenecks. Equally difficult was the full mobilisation of available resources. This required co-ordinated control and planning which looked to maximum efficiency in the recovery, allocation and use of resources. However, the nature of the Nazi state made this an idle dream. It was approached in the mid to late years of the war as a result of Speer's success in establishing some central direction of the war economy (Fig. 6.25), particularly in the quarterly allocation of primary materials like coal, iron and steel. Even then, however, deficiencies in the quantity and quality of labour remained to frustrate the position. There were also persistent weaknesses in transportation, not to mention the increasing effects of Allied bombing after 1942 which would have strained even the best co-ordinated of war economies. By 1942, Germany was in fact working a railway network in continental Europe which was almost two-thirds the size of that operated

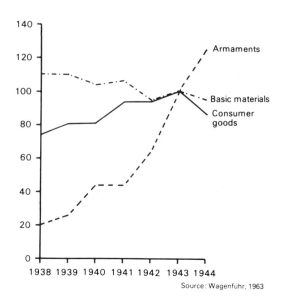

Source: Wagenführ, 1963

Source: Wagenführ, 1963

Fig. 6.25 (left) Index of total industrial production (1943 = 100)
Fig. 6.26 (right) Indices of major production groups (1943 = 100)

by the USA. This stretched the manpower resources of the Reichsbahn almost to breaking point; and there were parallel shortages of motive power and rolling stock. Russian broad-gauge tracks might be converted to narrow gauge relatively easily, but stock could not be so readily altered and resulted in limited resources being stretched over an even greater network. It is difficult to overestimate the functions of the railway system in wartime. It was the lifeline for the supply of armaments and stores to combat areas. It conveyed vital raw materials to Germany from occupied territories. Servicemen, labour conscripts, prisoners of war and concentration camp victims were all among the railways' traffic. Within Germany, the railways performed the vital task of servicing the complex industrial machine, particularly the high geographical concentration of activity in the Rhine–Ruhr, which, by definition, multiplied and elongated trade linkages and in so doing was to prove so devastating a handicap in the face of Allied bombing and, later, Allied invasion.

The requirements of war naturally made heavy additional demands upon basic industries like coal-mining, iron-working and steel manufacture (Fig. 6.26). Armaments production meanwhile brought with it a whole range of demands for non-ferrous metals; chromium, for example, was vital to the manufacture of armour plate, indeed of most alloy steels altogether. Also needed were oil supplies in growing quantities – for aviation spirit, carburettor and diesel fuel especially. Coal and lignite (brown coal) were materials in which Germany was fairly well endowed and the Nazis' territorial acquisitions added to this stock considerably. The lignite beds of Bohemia and Moravia, for instance, alone had an annual output of some 11 million tons. Within the *Altreich*, though, coal production barely increased at all over the course of the war. Production in 1938 was some 186 million tons; by 1943, it was only 190.4 million tons. Surprisingly little attention was given to coal planning, despite the build-up of coal-devouring branches of the chemical industry. In 1943, the annexed territories yielded an additional 88 million tons and the occupied areas a further 77 million. But the latter figure would have been yet higher had it proved possible to exploit the coal deposits of the Russian Donetz basin more rigorously. In total, it seems that the Nazis extracted less than a tenth of pre-war production levels in the Donetz. The real Achilles' heel of coal supply, however, was its dependence on railway transportation for distribution, and when the railway system became exposed to heavy air raids, that distribution broke down. This was notably true by the late autumn of 1944 and particularly affected the Ruhr, which provided some two-thirds of German output. In contrast to coal, there was a radical increase in lignite production within the *Altreich* – from 195 million tons in 1938 to 253.4 million by 1943. Most of this increase came from central Germany. The primary uses of lignite were for electricity generation and domestic heating.

Iron and steel

The raw material with which Germany was not well endowed, particularly for war production purposes, was iron ore (Fig. 6.27). The German ores were mostly low grade and low in phosophoric value, phosophorus content being important for armaments manufacture. Germany was traditionally a strong importer of quality iron ore, notably from Sweden. And since the Swedish ores were rich in phosophorus, they assumed vital significance in the German war economy, in some measure accounting for Hitler's 1940 campaign to secure the Norwegian flank. Nazi territorial annexation and conquest also brought significant spoils of iron ore. The Austrian reserves yielded an output of some 2 million tons at the time of annexation. But far greater were the reserves in the Lorraine region of France, with a pre-war yield of about 80 million tons.

The extent to which Nazi Germany came to depend on ore supplies from outside its 1937 borders is apparent in the accompanying diagrams. Discounting imports from neutral states, the figure was around 51 per cent in both 1943 and 1944. In 1943, in fact, only one-fifth of the Nazi empire's ore supply was accounted for by Germany proper. Over the course of the war, there was almost a 50 per cent drop in ore tonnage produced in the *Altreich*. The consequences of this external dependence in the face of Allied advances from east and west in 1944 were understandably acute. And with German prospects of winning the war receding rapidly, neutrals became less and less willing to maintain previous levels of ore supply.

Iron ore was transformed into a variety of ferrous products, but the most significant in terms of war economy were steels and steel plate. In 1937, raw steel output was just short of 20 million tons. By 1943, the Nazis had some 35 million at their disposal, roughly two thirds of which came from the *Altreich*, the remainder from the annexed and conquered territories. In the event, the demand for high grade steels and steel plate was never satisfied. There was a persistent shortfall which stemmed fundamentally from deficient production capacity, not deficient material availability. This reflected a basic

Fig. 6.27 Sources of iron
ore, 1940–44

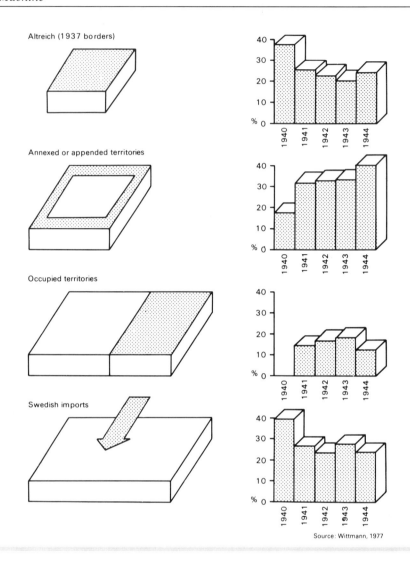

Altreich (1937 borders)

Annexed or appended territories

Occupied territories

Swedish imports

Source: Wittmann, 1977

lack of plant investment in the inter-war period and the general reluctance of
the Nazi economic leadership to maintain such manufacturing capacity
beyond the borders of Greater Germany where it was not only less secure,
but more open to SS domination and manipulation.

Other metals

Steel production problems were reinforced by increasing difficulties over the
supply of chromium. For these, Nazi Germany relied heavily on neutral
Turkey and Albania. Turkey in 1943 supplied almost 5,000 tons, roughly
double the production of Greater Germany and the occupied territories put
together. The figure rose to nearly 12,000 tons in 1944. The enforced
German withdrawal from south-east Europe interfered with chrome supplies,
both in their acquisition and in their carriage to Germany itself.

Aluminium was another material vital to the German war effort, notably for aircraft production. Soon after the occupation of Norway in 1940, plans were laid to create a massively enlarged aluminium industry there, making use of the large and cheap supplies of hydro-electricity. Norway had no bauxite reserves, though. These had to be imported from France and Hungary; and herein lay the weak link of production plans, that is aside from the costs and manpower requirements of constructing eight new hydro-electric power stations and 10 new smelting plants.

Oil supplies

Of all Nazi Germany's material demands, however, the greatest challenges and the greatest difficulties were presented in oil supply. In perspective, the response was an impressive one (Figs 6.28 and 6.29). With limited supplies of mineral oil within its borders, synthetic oil production had been a feature of the industry since the mid-1920s, and by the middle years of the war output was roughly five times that of mineral oil. Even before the outbreak of war, Germany had achieved the largest synthetic oil industry in the world, despite failures to meet plan targets. Austria yielded mineral oil to Nazi Germany, as did various other annexed or occupied territories. But the bulk of the remaining deficit was met by Rumanian mineral oil production. By 1941, nearly 3 million tons were being imported for German use and for the active armed forces. This compared with 2.5 million tons of synthetic production.

Throughout the early years of the war, there were minor difficulties over oil supplies – related, for example, to transportation problems, irregularities

Source: Wagenführ, 1963

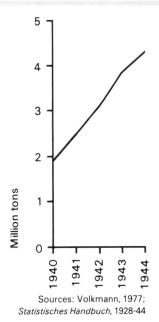

Sources: Volkmann, 1977;
Statistisches Handbuch, 1928-44

Fig. 6.28 (left) Mineral oil supply
Fig. 6.29 (right) Synthetic oil production (Greater Germany)

Fig. 6.30 Aviation, carburettor and diesel fuel production, 1944–45

Source: Wagenführ, 1963

of demand and diverse jurisdictional conflicts within the Nazi organisation. But these were nothing compared to the havoc wrought by Allied bombing from the spring of 1944. In the view of some commentators, this became the most serious single threat to the German war economy.

Synthetic oil capacity, concentrated as it was in the Ruhr and in the central industrial belt, proved a relatively easy target. Some two-thirds of the hydrogenation capacity was actually contained within only seven plants. The impact of bombing on fuel production is demonstrated in the accompanying graph (Fig. 6.30). Aviation fuel output, the bulk of which derived from synthetic production, dropped catastrophically. As the need for fighter protection against bombing raids on the plants grew, so the raids were progressively destroying the fighters' own fuel. Reconstruction work was pressed with all speed but barely kept ahead of renewed attacks. From the summer of 1944 onwards, therefore, Hitler's Reich and the armed forces in particular faced critical fuel shortages. This could not fail to hasten the pace of defeat.

The supply of food

By the last winter of the war, food supplies had also been reduced to a critical level; the average daily calorie intake for civilians was below the minimum considered necessary for long-term survival (1,800 per day). Until that time, however, Nazi Germany had been relatively well provided with food especially when set against the chronic food shortages suffered in the later years of the First World War. Rationing was instituted immediately the war broke out in 1939 and remained effective up to 1943/4, when black marketing began to assume growing signifiance in the face of contracting official allocations. The most serious set-back to food supply was probably that occasioned by the severe winter of 1941/2 which destroyed much winter grain and damaged potato crops and stores. Occupied territories yielded grain and other food commodities (Fig. 6.31). Indeed, the decision to drive

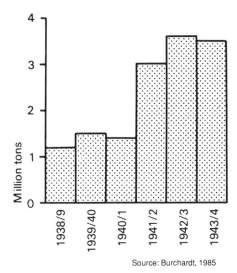

Fig. 6.31 Bread grains from occupied territories

Million tons

1938/9 1939/40 1940/1 1941/2 1942/3 1943/4

Source: Burchardt, 1985

the German attack on Russia south-east to the Ukraine in summer 1941 was ostensibly to secure the rich food resources of that region. In fact, the greater part of the Russian grain harvest collected by the Germans went to supply the army. And in spite of instituting one of the most vicious occupational regimes, German rule in Russia actually yielded a limited reward. It is estimated, for example, that net German imports in agriculture totalled only 3,500 million Reichsmarks, a fraction of what the Nazi state obtained from France alone. The scale of bread grain imports to the Reich from occupied territories is illustrated in the accompanying diagram (Fig. 6.31). By 1942/3, they met just short of a third of demand. The pattern for meat and fat was not dissimilar. The steady attrition of Hitler's land conquests from 1943 inevitably spelt a progressive diminution in these food supplies. And the position was made doubly difficult by the need to supply the armed forces at the front from German sources, where previously they had subsisted directly from the territories under occupation.

42   *The supply of men*

The civilian labour force in Germany fell from 39.1 million to 28.4 million between May 1939 and September 1944 (Fig. 6.32). In a country which was already experiencing a labour crisis in 1938/9, the consequences for the operation of the war economy were severe. Nor was it simply a question of deficient numbers. The quality of the labour force became equally problematic. The pace at which workers could be trained in vital industrial skills became steadily inadequate as armament production accelerated. Wehrmacht conscription added to the difficulties. Even early on in the war, newly trained young men were liable to call-up; and emergency drafting in later years probed yet more widely into the profile of skilled labour. By the

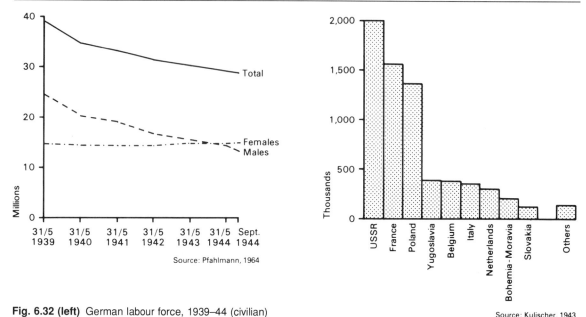

Source: Pfahlmann, 1964

Fig. 6.32 (left) German labour force, 1939–44 (civilian)

Fig. 6.33 (right) Sources of foreign labour, early 1943 (estimates in thousands, including POWs)

Source: Kulischer, 1943

autumn of 1944, in fact, some 13 million had been called up, while the number of those lost in combat totalled 3.9 million.

For reasons examined earlier, there was little mobilisation of women to make up for the losses to the civilian labour force. Indeed, in the first two years of war, there was a fall in female labour strength. However, the regime was very effective in adding to its labour force by drafting in foreign workers from occupied or allied countries and by utilising prisoners of war (Fig. 6.33). The latter soon became part of a massive, inhumane slave labour programme. By spring 1941 there were some 1.5 million foreign workers engaged in Germany, and in some Labour Ministry regions they represented over 10 per cent of the workforce (Fig. 6.34). At the same time, there were just over 1 million employed POWs. By early 1943, the figures had risen to 4.8 million foreign workers and 1.75 million POWs. But even though the total foreign and POW labour force may have reached nearly 8 million, this was still short of replacement level. Moreover, POW labour was no substitute, man for man, for ordinary labour, a feature compounded by appalling living conditions in the POW camps.

For Himmler and the SS, such camps were a means of achieving Nazi racial goals. During the first years of the war with Russia, roughly 2 million Russian POWs perished on the eastern front – deliberately annihilated through a combination of starvation rations and forced labour. Russians were near the bottom of the Nazi racial hierarchy, their plight compounded by the 'menace' of Bolshevism. The Reich Labour Ministry, while not dissenting from the concept of a racial hierarchy, nevertheless saw foreign labour in a more permanent role within a German-dominated Europe. *Gastarbeiter* were seen as a necessary feature of the Nazi empire, not just in dealing with the labour demands of war but in accommodating more substantive structural

Fig. 6.34 Foreign labour in the workforce, 25 April 1941

Note: regions are those of the Reich Labour Ministry. POWs are included.

Foreign labour in
the workforce
25 April 1941

Percentage

■	Over 13.0
⊘	10.1-13.0
⊞	7.6-10.0
▥	6.6-7.5
⊟	5.1-6.5
☰	4.1-5.0
⋯	4.0 and under

Source: Pfahlmann, 1964

I	East Prussia	IX	Hesse	XVII	Upper Danube
II	Pomerania	X	Saxony	(XVIII)	Bohemia (n.d.)
III	Nordmark	XI	Silesia	XIX	Sudentenland
IV	Lower Saxony	XII	Sudetenland	(XX)	Moravia (n.d.)
V	Brandenburg	XIII	Zwgst. Nuremberg	XXI	Vienna–Lower Danube
VI	Middle Germany	XIV	Westmark	XXII	Steiermark–Kärnten
VII	Westphalia	XV	South-West Germany	XXIII	Alpenland
VIII	Rhineland	XVI	Bavaria		

problems in the labour market. Even so, pay and conditions were graded according to racial dogma, Western Europeans being treated much like ordinary Germans, those from Eastern Europe as an under-class. Despite the relative pragmatism of the Labour Ministry, though, foreign labour was often used inappropriately. Skilled men were employed in non-skilled positions, especially in agriculture. More generally, muscle power took precedence over trade skill.

The efficiency of wartime labour utilisation became a particular worry for Albert Speer and his armaments ministry. The central powers that Speer managed to assemble over raw material allocation, weapon supply to the different services, and the organisation of production never extended to labour. In 1942, this became the province of a General Plenipotentiary for Labour, Fritz Sauckel, former Gauleiter of Thuringia. Sauckel enjoyed rather similar central powers and was able to streamline and speed up the movement and allocation of labour, particularly that from occupied territories. In four recruiting campaigns from spring 1942 to December 1944, he procured over 5 million foreigners and POWs. But Sauckel's relationship with the Speer ministry was an uneasy one; and it deteriorated steadily as prospects of defeat loomed. Speer argued for the retention of industrial workers in occupied areas as the most effective means of maximising armaments output. Sauckel differed, and in January 1944, for example, won Hitler's sanction for the deporting of roughly a million French workmen to the Reich over the course of that year. As a long-standing Party figure, he belonged to a group who were suspicious of the role occupied by the business interests with which Speer's ministry was inextricably bound. And the antipathy developed a mutual character as industrialists increasingly perceived financial ruin as the only outcome of total defeat.

43   *Civilian conditions*

Two factors were critical to the determination of civilian conditions in wartime Germany. The first was the uncompromising desire to avoid what Germany had experienced in the First World War, when food supplies declined drastically, the cost of living rose much more quickly than incomes, and soldiers' families, in particular, were reduced to the barest of subsistence levels. The second was the National Socialists' need to maintain the support of the population at large. As a novel and radical regime, it relied on the general acquiescence of the people to maintain some degree of stability; there was not the innate stability that existed in Britain. The outcome was that, until the later years of the war, Nazi Germany did not experience the full rigours of war economy (Fig. 6.35). The pre-war level of consumer goods production, for example, was maintained to a considerably greater degree than in Britain. Assigning the value of 100 to the base year of 1938, British production had fallen to 81 by 1941, German to only 97. Even as late as the fifth year of the war, some 43 per cent of those employed in Nazi Germany were engaged on tasks for civilian consumption. Speer's Ministry

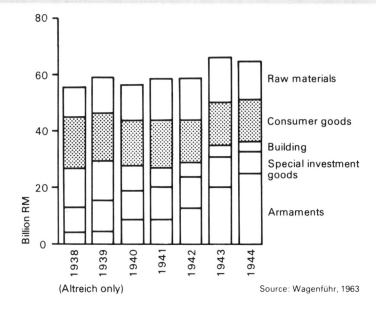

Fig. 6.35 Consumer goods in relation to other production sectors: 1933–44 (1943 prices)

(Altreich only)   Source: Wagenführ, 1963

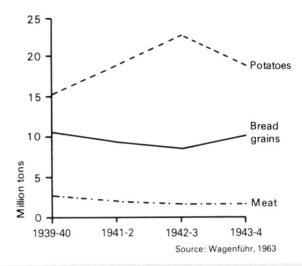

Fig. 6.36 Consumption of important foodstuffs

Source: Wagenführ, 1963

fought hard to reduce the level in favour of war production. It was really successful only in the textile sector, where production of men's clothing, for instance, fell some 80 per cent from 1943 to 1944.

Food rationing was adopted in Germany immediately upon the outbreak of war, with differentiations made for regional food preferences. This, coupled with fair grain stocks, sufficient labour and fertiliser allocations, and imports, contributed to a reasonably stable food situation until all but the last months of the war. Predictably, given Germany's pre-war agricultural pattern, there were cutbacks in meat and fat supplies, but consumption of bread grains and potatoes was more than maintained up to 1944 (Fig. 6.36).

The cost-of-living index increased by only 12 per cent during the course of the war and was nearly matched by the increase in wages. This was achieved by state control of prices and wages, and assisted by the relatively favourable supply positions in food and other goods. Given that rationing prevailed, however, many Germans found themselves with more money than they could spend. The institution of a wide-ranging and relatively generous set of payments to families of serving men tended to reinforce the pattern.

Another significant contrast between the German and British war economies was in the use of women for war work. This was instituted in Britain at an early stage and proved a vital supplement to the labour force. In Nazi Germany, the employment of women was objected to on a variety of grounds, including concern for soldiers' morale. What is more, the favourable financial supports given by National Socialism to 'the family' resulted in an outflow of women from employment. Speer's ministry reckoned that between July 1939 and February 1942, some 80,000 left *industrial* employment to stay at home. Over the entire course of the war, the total number of women in the labour force remained static at about 14.5 million. This has to be set alongside the increasing demands of the armed forces draft, which, after two and a half years of war, had absorbed some 7.5 million men.

Civilian existence in wartime Germany, then, was not a harsh one, except for political dissidents and racial outcasts. However, this became less and less true from 1943 as Allied bombers started to raze the face of many German cities and as the death toll of the *Wehrmacht* climbed. In the last years of the Russian campaign, whole army divisions were almost wiped out, leaving few German families unaffected. Ultimately, there were 3.5 million dead servicemen.

44   *German resistance to National Socialism*

Assessments of resistance within the Third Reich face formidable problems of interpretation. Major incidents such as the von Stauffenberg bomb plot of 20 July 1944 and earlier army attempts either to arrest or assassinate Hitler are clear enough testament (Fig. 6.37), but resistance at grass-roots level is not nearly so easily apprehended or appraised. It is represented in the detainees in concentration camps from the regime's earliest days, in arrests for political crimes, in seizures of 'illegal' literature, and in various forms of unco-operative action and non-conformist behaviour. Some commentators have been lead to distinguish between resistance (*Widerstand*) as organised action in rejection of the regime and resistance (*Resistenz*) as opposition or dissent which found expression in different degrees of immunity to the regime's totalising policies. Much of the antagonism of the churches to Nazism may be construed in the latter sense. More everyday examples of *Resistenz* were failure to offer the 'Heil Hitler' salute, listening to foreign radio broadcasts after it had become illegal to do so from September 1939, and subscribing to youth cultures that were perceived by the regime as

Fig. 6.37 Principal locations of resistance to National Socialism, 1933–45

For reasons given above, a map of 'set-piece' incidents of this kind can be misleading. But it does show that resistance was relatively widespread rather than geographically confined.

Principal locations of resistance to National Socialism 1933-45

• Civilian resistance

▽ Church resistance

▲ Military resistance

0   200
km

Source: Aleff, n.d.

un-German. It is extraordinarily difficult to evaluate this second type of resistance. Some of the non-conformists, for example, later became active in organised resistance, particularly as the regime became progressively more radicalised. There is a sense, in other words, in which resistance must be seen as process; and thus it may be that analytical distinctions of the kind represented by *Widerstand* and *Resistenz* have the potential to be misleading. A wider problem of assessment is the fact that non-conformist behaviour, and even organised protest, could be the province of individuals or groups who actually assented to certain of the regime's policies. A further difficulty is the way non-conformity or protest could sometimes be enmeshed with other, much deeper currents of social change: for instance, the evolving class relations under an increasingly monopolistic industrial capitalism.

Organised German resistance can be conveniently separated into two camps: that of the conservatives or right wing, largely represented by leading members of the army and of the German elite; and that of the left wing in which the outlawed German Communist Party (KPD) dominated. The strength of communist opposition within the broader frame of left-wing resistance is demonstrated in the available statistics. In 1936, for example, some 11,700 were arrested as against only 1,400 for the Social Democratic Party (SPD) and associate groups. The adjacent graph for 1938–9 replicates the pattern (Fig. 6.38). The conclusion of a Nazi–Soviet pact in August 1939 naturally stemmed the force of communist opposition. But after the invasion of Russia in June 1941, it again gathered momentum, especially as reflected in the communist press (Fig. 6.39). Communist arrests in 1941 totalled over 11,000, almost a return to the level of 1936 (Fig. 6.40). Ultimately, though, the communists had limited success in uniting or mobilising the working classes at large in opposition to Nazism. In effect, the KPD became an opposition in waiting, its ambitions realised only when Stalin's armies had over-run large parts of Hitler's Reich.

The conservative opposition in which members of the army figured strongly, was best placed of all Nazi political opponents to achieve positive

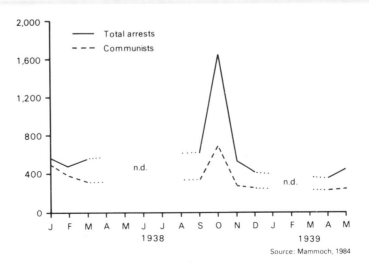

Fig. 6.38 Arrests for political resistance, 1938–39

Source: Mammoch, 1984

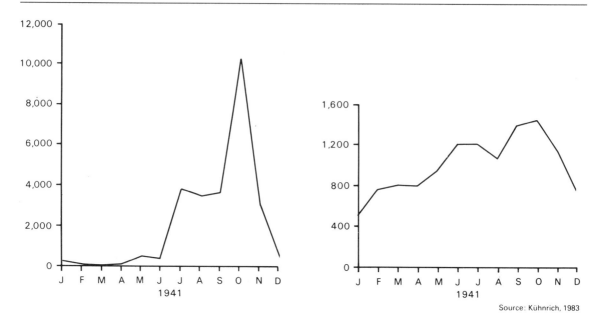

Source: Kühnrich, 1983

Fig. 6.39 Gestapo seizures of Communist fly-sheets and newspapers in 1941
Fig. 6.40 Arrests on account of Communist and Marxist activities in 1941

results, but it laboured under one very important shadow: the cause of patriotism. In France, resistance could hardly be construed as anything but patriotic. In Germany the synonymity was non-existent. When Hitler's policies were winning, resistance looked like treason. For this reason a number of serious army plots to arrest Hitler ultimately evaporated due to lack of support. This was notably true in the crisis over the Sudetenland and in the subsequent capitulation of the western powers to Hitler's demands. The startling successes of the German armies first in Poland, then in Scandinavia, and later in western Europe, dampened the force and conviction of military opposition yet further. Not until 1942, when the tide of war was beginning to move in favour of the Allies, was activity renewed. It culminated in the abortive July 1944 *coup* when Hitler survived a bomb placed in his East Prussian headquarters at Rastenburg. This plot had been preceded by several others which had sought (unsuccessfully) to eliminate Hitler. Its failure was followed by a ruthless Nazi vendetta, which was soon to liquidate a major part of the conservative opposition, including most of the members of the Kreisau Circle, a remarkable resistance group which subscribed to liberal principles and had been secretly deliberating on the nature of a post-Hitler Germany.

It is conceivable that the activities of the conservative opposition in the last years of the war might have been enhanced had it not been for the policy of unconditional surrender formulated by the Allies as early as 1943. In such a context, *any* attempt to wrest power away from the Nazi leadership faced a formidable problem of credibility in the eyes of ordinary Germans. But beyond all such considerations, it is impossible to escape the simple fact of Nazi terror, imagined as well as real. For large sections of the German

Fig. 6.41 Nazi view of distribution of Jews in Europe circa 1935

This map should be viewed as a characteristic piece of Nazi propaganda. It is misleading rather than inaccurate, as the map in section one of Part Three has already shown. In reality, Jewish populations were heavily concentrated in towns and cities.

Source: *Historischer Schul-Atlas*, 1935 (BA Koblenz)

people, passive grumbling became the commonest way in which resistance was displayed. And given the honeycombing of society by Nazi activists, the articulation of such grievances into organised dissent was readily intercepted.

45 *The Holocaust*

If there is any one single act for which the Nazis will be remembered, it is the systematic extermination of the Jews of Europe (Fig. 6.41). Even today, almost 50 years later, the 'Holocaust' remains a subject of intense debate and dispute in the western world at large and in Germany itself. Indeed, in the mid-1980s, there erupted within West German academia what subsequently became known as the *Historikerstreit* (historical battle or quarrel) when question marks were placed over the assumed singularity or incomparability of the Nazi annihilation of Jews, in part as an attempt to historicise the Nazi past, to cope with the way in which that past appeared in some eyes to remain as powerful as the present, encapsulated in the phrase 'the past that will not pass'. The vigorous and, at times, bitter controversy that followed was played out in the German press in full public view. It revealed, above all, that interpretations of the Holocaust continue to be beset by problems of political and emotional engagement, even where commentators have no obvious connection with the reality of the events. In 1994, the screening in German cinemas of Stephen Spielberg's epic film, *Schindler's List*, added a further milestone. In balancing horror with humanity, in telling the story of how a Nazi industrialist rescued more than a thousand Jews from certain death, it challenged Germans to ask themselves why others did not do something, why so many Germans were bystanders.

There is no reliable figure for the number of Jews who perished in Nazi hands, nor for the other racial and social 'undesirables' who fell to the same lot, including the Sinti and Roma, or 'gypsies'. Estimates of total Jewish deaths range between 4 million and 6 million. Perhaps a quarter of these lost their lives at the hands of the *Einsatzgruppen*, particularly in Poland and in

Russia. The rest were shot or gassed in notorious death camps like Auschwitz, or else worked to death in servitude to the SS.

The war saw a progressive barbarisation of Nazi policies towards the Jews – not as a result of a clearly laid out plan, but as a function of conflicting objectives among the various Nazi power blocs which found resolution only in more and more radical measures. Emigration ceased and large numbers of the Jewish populations of Germany, Austria and the newly conquered parts of Poland were rounded up and shipped to the areas of Poland not incorporated in the Greater German Reich, the so-called 'remainder state', or Polish Government-General. Here they were 'concentrated' in ghettos, the largest being Lodz (established February 1940) and Warsaw (established November 1940). The area south of Lublin also became a major reception zone for Jewish deportees, and for some months in 1940 the intention was that this would become a reservation for Europe's entire Jewish population. Once in the Polish ghettos, the Jews became slave labourers, working in poor conditions and with inadequate food.

The genesis of the final solution to the Jewish question and the seat of its responsibility have been the focus of exceptionally intense investigation. The direct role of Hitler is not readily identified. However, there can be no doubting the way his maniacal hatred of the Jews permeated not only the SS, but the state, the Party and the army. It gave legitimation to the last steps in the barbarisation of policy towards the Jews as the various power blocs of the Third Reich grappled with the thousands of Jewish men, women and children who were daily converging upon the Polish territories and for whom, with stalemate on the Russian front, the prospect of survival in a slave state in the East appeared increasingly remote.

Full-scale genocide began in Russia in the wake of the advancing German armies. The *Einsatzgruppen* assembled by Himmler and Heydrich to liquidate leading Bolsheviks, subsequently extended their mandate to Russia's Jews. Thus within months of the opening of the Barbarossa campaign of 22 June 1941, some 600,000 had been killed. A second major phase of killing opened in the spring of 1942.

For those Jews in Poland and the remainder of occupied Europe, including those still in Germany performing vital munitions work, a more thorough method of liquidation was sought. Gas had been used by the Nazis between 1938 and 1941 in connection with the euthanasia experiments for the mentally handicapped and chronically sick. Some of the staff involved in that programme were transferred to assist in dealing with the Jews and to help set up gas chambers for mass killing (Fig. 6.42). Hitler probably decided upon a policy of systematic genocide in the late summer of 1941. The first extermination camp was opened at Chelmno within the borders of Greater Germany in December 1941. Further camps followed at Belzec in the Polish Government-General (opened March 1942), at Sobibor on the border between the Government-General and the Reichskommissariat Ukraine (opened May 1942), and at Treblinka, north-east of Warsaw (opened July 1942). To these four camps must be added two existing concentration and labour camps which were subsequently equipped with extermination facilities: Lublin and Auschwitz.

Over the course of 1942 and 1943, the Nazi campaign against the Jews

Fig. 6.42 The death camps

was accelerated. Satellite states in south-east Europe were increasingly drawn into it, while in western occupied zones Jews were steadily rounded up preparatory to railway transportation east (Fig. 6.43). Jews still performing vital munitions work in Berlin and in areas like the Polish Government-General were similarly evacuated. The fact that neither their labour nor their skills could be adequately replaced was immaterial in the eyes of Himmler and other Nazi fanatics like Goebbels. Thus developed some of the bitterest internal rivalries of the Nazi regime. At a time when Speer and all the various representatives of his armaments ministry were seeking to maximise war production, Himmler and the SS were depleting the labour force, absorbing vital railway capacity and consuming precious building materials in the making of their camp installations. Given the primacy of the SS in occupied Europe, especially in the east, it was the crusade to wipe out the Jewish race rather than victory in war which generally held sway.

Auschwitz became the biggest of the extermination camps, as well as providing workforces for numerous SS enterprises. Mass transports of Jews began arriving there in March 1942. By late autumn of 1944, as many as two million Jews may have perished there – either worked to death, shot, gassed, or killed in grotesque medical experiments by SS doctors invariably undertaken without any form of anaesthetic.

Auschwitz's one-time camp commandant, Rudolf Hoess, became the

Fig. 6.43
Deportation of
Jews from
France, the
Low Countries,
Italy and
Greece:
1942–44

Nazis' ultimate technocrat of death. His advocacy of Zyklon-B crystals (hydrogen cyanide) as the most efficient method of gassing is by now infamous. In the earlier euthanasia experiments and in the lesser extermination camps, carbon monoxide was used. Hoess maintained that Zyklon-B was quicker and more efficient. And as it was already used in the camps as a fumigant, there were few problems of obtaining additional supplies. One Hamburg chemical firm was eventually to supply Auschwitz with two tons of the crystals a month. Auschwitz also had a physical capacity for extermination which outstripped its sister camps. At Treblinka, the 10 gas chambers accommodated only 200 each. Hoess built five chambers each capable of accommodating 2000 and in his testimony at Nuremberg reckoned that up to 16,000 camp inmates were processed daily. Auschwitz was also distinguised from several of the other extermination centres in the way it sought to disguise the gas chambers and the associated

Fig. 6.44
The murder of Europe's Jewish population

The murder of Europe's Jewish population

Estimated percentages

76-100

51-75

26-50

0-25

Borders as in 1937

HOLLAND

BELGIUM

GERMANY

FRANCE

ITALY

CZECHOSLOVAKIA

AUSTRIA

HUNGARY

YUGOSLAVIA

POLAND

LATVIA

LITHUANIA

USSR

RUMANIA

BULGARIA

GREECE

0   200
km

Source: Noakes and Pridham, 1984

crematoria – with the aid of gardens, for example. However, even Hoess's zealous pursuit of the speediest and most efficent machinery of death failed in the handling of the dead bodies. The crematoria proved incapable of disposing of the corpses fast enough.

Throughout their deliberations over the Jewish race, Nazi leaders sought to maintain a cloak of secrecy, particularly as the policy of large-scale physical extermination became a reality. The language of euphemism as seen in terms like 'final solution' and 'special treatment' was one symptom of the trend. But Heydrich, Himmler's deputy in the overseeing of the Jewish question, soon realised that more concrete disguise would be necessary given the sheer scale of the extermination and the many Reich and SS agencies which would inevitably become involved. One of his principal solutions was the setting up of a special Jewish ghetto at Theresienstadt in northern Bohemia. It was intended for Jews over 65 years of age, the inmates having first been persuaded to make over their assets to the Reich Association of Jews in return for housing, food and welfare.

Theresienstadt subsequently became a propaganda stage for the Nazis' treatment of Jews. The camp was emphasised as being humane. Photographic records were released which showed senior Jews engaging in self-government. Even a Red Cross inspection was arranged in an attempt to convince ordinary Germans as well as the wider world of the sincerity of the enterprise. In reality, of course, Theresienstadt proved very close to being a concentration camp. And above all it operated as a transit centre for the death camps further east.

If the whole ghastly programme of Jewish extermination was instituted by Hitler and his closest Nazi leaders and the genocide act itself carried out by the regime's elite guard, it remains true that thousands of ordinary Germans knew what was happening and many thousands more had a good general idea of the Nazis' treatment of the Jews. The Wehrmacht had extensive, often first-hand, knowledge, particularly in the case of the *Einsatzgruppen* operating in Russia in the rear of advancing army groups. Railway employees involved in the mass transit of Jews to the extermination camps knew that human bodies were being incinerated there. Auschwitz, moreover, was on the borders of the heavily popoulated industrial area of Upper Silesia. There were ordinary Germans in the factories associated with the concentration camps there, notably those of the IG-Farben combine; and the smoke and stench from the crematoria were evident for miles around. Some were revolted by what they witnessed themselves or learned about second-hand; some closed their eyes and sought refuge in Nazi racial propaganda; many knew but simply did not believe.

Epilogue

Epilogue

The *Hitler state* ceased to exist when the *Führer* committed suicide in his Berlin bunker on 30 April 1945, although Admiral Doenitz, Hitler's chosen successor, tried in vain to prolong the Third Reich's existence from his headquarters at Flensburg on the Danish border. The policy of the Allies towards a defeated Germany had been set out as early as January 1943 at the Casablanca conference. It called for Germany's unconditional surrender and the occupation of all German territory for an undefined period. The territorial losses sustained by Germany's neighbours from 1937 were to be rectified and the entire German war machine dismantled.

The actual occupation of Germany from April 1945 involved a four-power division among the USSR, the USA, Britain and France; Greater Berlin, located deep inside the Soviet zone became a four-power city, with access for the western powers along specially defined routes (Fig. E.1). From the start, native Germans were permitted a considerable measure of administrative autonomy, although this did not prevent the four powers from pursuing distinctive general occupation policies, especially in the Soviet area where Stalinist ideology invariably prevailed. Subsequently, this divergence sharpened, and coupled with a steady deterioration in relations between the Soviets and the Western Allies, became the stage-set for the emergence of two separate German states by 1949: the Federal Republic in the British, French and United States zones; the Democratic Republic in the Soviet zone.

German suffering in the immediate post-war years was great. In 1945, national income per capita was down to less than a quarter of the pre-war level; even by 1948 it had risen to only two-thirds. There was chronic economic dislocation and there were desperate housing shortages in the many bombed cities. Problems also arose from the quadripartite occupation system. The malfunctioning of the German state was great enough from physical destruction of its fabric, without introducing arbitrary geographical divides. This applied particularly in the movement of food. However, the most potent indicator of the German plight was the problem of expellees. The annexation by Poland and the USSR of parts of the pre-war German Reich, together with the untenable position of ethnic Germans beyond the Reich's pre-war borders, precipitated a massive westward flight of refugees. By 1960, as many as 12 million people may have figured in this largely forced migration, while several million more perished in the process of

Fig. E.1 Occupied Germany, 1945–49

Occupied Germany 1945-9

- – · – Borders of postwar Germany
- – – – Borders of four-power occupation zones
- Soviet zone
- British zone
- American zone
- French zone
- Territory lost to Poland and USSR

Source: Hilgemann, 1984

expulsion. In many parts of north Germany, eastern refugees came to form major components of the total population. In Mecklenburg, 42.5 per cent of the population were expellees in 1946.

Economic hardships and the severance of so many Germans from their homelands were obvious enough foci for renewed political extremism. And in spite of extensive de-nazification and re-education by the Western Allied powers, right-wing nationalism remained alive in western Germany, in later years making only the barest of attempts to disguise its Nazi inspiration and connections. Indeed, the NPD (National Democratic Party) was to become labelled by liberal opponents the NSDAP without the SA. But there was one vital facet of the first post-war decades which distinguished them from Weimar: the so-called West German economic miracle. From 1949, the Federal Republic sustained an extraordinarily rapid economic recovery – such that the gibe of the man in the street became: 'we may have lost the war but we won the peace'. It consistently outperformed its European partners and became a linchpin of the post-war Western European economic system. Recovery in the Democratic Republic was more strained and produced a steady migration of people to the Federal Republic through the 'safety valve' of Berlin. This was halted, however, with the erection of the Berlin Wall in August 1961, which sealed off the old Soviet sector from the West, creating a divided city. Henceforward the Democratic Republic attained a greater measure of stability and prosperity. In political terms, however, it became a steadily more entrenched member of the 'eastern block' and stand-off with the Federal Republic, particularly over West Berlin, formed one of the most potent symbols of the 'Cold War'.

From the 1970s, the scale of tension between the two states eased as the two governments searched for co-operative positions, particularly over economic, humanitarian and defence matters. Behind this pragmatic facade, though, the ideological stances remained fixed: for the Federal Republic's leadership, co-operation was conceived as part of a step-by-step programme towards the ultimate goal of re-unification, however distant that prospect appeared; for the Democratic Republic in the east, on the other hand, co-operation signalled increasing recognition and acceptance of its legitimacy as an independent state.

On this basis, then, the division of Germany, even in the mid-1980s, seemed immutable. Among the most sanguine commentators, prospects of there ever again being a united Germany were viewed as remote. However, events were soon to prove otherwise. Within the extraordinary space of just 15 months over 1989 and 1990, the German Democratic Republic collapsed. By October 1990, there were no longer two separate German states: a new unified state, numbering some 78 million souls, had come into being. This astonishing transformation came about largely through a popular revolution. The balance among East Germans between public conformity and private dissent finally snapped in the late summer of 1989. As a result, there emerged a remarkable democratic awakening – in a state which had known no democratic voice for almost 60 years.

This extraordinary pattern was set in train with a rising tide of illegal emigration to the Federal Republic, especially via the eastern block state of Hungary. When confronted by the government of the German Democratic Republic, the Hungarian government broke ranks from its Warsaw pact partner and opted to open the border for the fleeing refugees. Thus was the infamous 'Iron Curtain' drawn. Moreover, the reform climate in Moscow, under Gorbachev, ruled out Soviet interference. The response of the East German regime under its hard-line communist leader, Erich Honecker, was to cut off travel to Hungary for its citizens. But this merely redirected flight through Czechoslovakia and Poland where would-be emigrants sought refuge in West German embassy compounds. After some interim concessions, the communist leadership sought a further suspension of travel permits, only to see the tide of popular dissent re-double in its force. Years of pent-up frustration over travel restrictions, coupled with widespread resentment at the regime's failure to engage in the reform process underway elsewhere in Eastern Europe, along with rising dissatisfaction over the growing gap between socialist rhetoric and the everyday reality of living conditions, brought a wave of street protest. The Saxon city of Leipzig, in particular, became the key stage on which confrontation with the authorities was played out.

The initial reaction of the communist authorities to such popular protest was an increase in the use of police force, but the crowds refused to be intimidated. As protest spread to other cities, sections of the communist authorities sought dialogue not bloodshed and this provided the cue for a dramatic unfolding of political opposition encompassing left as well as right. Even the hitherto rigidly controlled media responded to the political ferment and began openly criticising Honecker's regime.

In the opening week of October 1989, the Democratic Republic celebrated its 40th anniversary and its leader regaled thousands of foreign dignitaries with his regime's achievements. Within a matter of days, however, Honecker had been unceremoniously ousted, his mantle assumed by a more flexible apparatchik, Egon Krenz. In a desperate bid to seize the political initiative, Krenz sought a rapid reform agenda, including a new travel law. When this failed to stay the tide of popular protest, the regime gambled on opening the Berlin Wall on 9 November. But rather than courting popularity, this merely served to give even freer rein to popular passions. And these were underscored as the international community shared in the destruction of the 'Cold War's' most potent reminder and as the West German Chancellor, Helmut Kohl, bore down upon the political vacuum in the east with plans for unity. The result was that, by December, Krenz had resigned and the East German politburo and Communist Party Central Committee had dissolved themselves.

Residual power now lay with the moderate communist Prime Minister, Hans Modrow, who became the focus of a search for a new socialism, a last-ditch attempt by the Communist Party to save face. Once more, however, the government proved hopelessly out of step with the tide of popular resentment. Incensed by a move to scale down but still retain in some form the infamous Stasi, or secret police, protesters stormed the Stasi headquarters compound in East Berlin demanding the organisation's complete dissolution. In parallel, Modrow's government was having to cope with mounting economic difficulties which brought fully into the public eye the economic failures under the planned economy. Pressed by the forces of political opposition, previously proposed free elections were brought forward to the spring of 1990. The expectation was that the newly formed Social Democratic Party would be the victor. The actual decision of the voters, however, was momentous. They chose the Christian Democratic Alliance.

In effect, this was a decision for unification, since six weeks before the election Chancellor Kohl had been instrumental in forging this particular combination of centre-right political groupings in the Democratic Republic and was to become its most powerful platform speaker. With such simple slogans as 'freedom and unity', the Alliance won almost 50 per cent of the popular vote. The people's verdict left the Democratic Republic in ruins and unification became largely a matter of time. The four leading international actors in the post-war division of Germany, namely the USSR, the USA, Britain and France, eventually bowed to the inevitable. The currencies of the two Germanies were amalgamated on 1 July 1990 and full political union followed on 2 October 1990. The old Democratic Republic became the five new *Bundesländer*; state and *Bundestag* elections quickly followed.

If German division had been one of the most powerful legacies of National Socialism, unification might be seen to have finally extinguished its spectre. There are senses, however, in which this is too hasty a conclusion. The enlarged German state has invited comparisons with Hitler's Reich, for example. More problematical for Germans themselves is the rediscovered

Fig. E.2 Unified Germany, 1990

Unified
Germany
1990

0   100 km

Mecklenburg-
Vorpommern

Brandenburg

Berlin

Sachsen-
Anhalt

Thüringen

Sachsen

Source: Bodleian

sense of nationalism which the events of 1989 and 1990 brought; in these terms, the continuities with Hitler's Reich are hard to escape.

References for maps and diagrams

Unpublished sources

BA Koblenz: Bundesarchiv Koblenz.

Bodleian: Bodleian Library, University of Oxford.

OUSOG: Oxford University School of Geography Library.

Official published sources: German

Die Kunst im Dritten Reich: monthly Nazi periodical devoted to all forms of art and to architecture.

Der nationalsozialistische Schulungsbrief: monthly Nazi periodical devoted to education and schools.

Statistisches Jahrbuch: annual statistical yearbook.

Wirtschaft und Statistik: monthly digest of economic commentary, including statistics.

Official published sources: British, United States and Allied

Adm Hbk: HMSO 1944–5 British Admiralty Handbooks for Germany (4 vols). London – produced by Naval Intelligence Division based at the University of Cambridge.

Germany Basic Handbook: HMSO 1944–5 Economic surveys for the British Foreign Office and Ministry of Economic Warfare (21 vols). London.

Serial Maps: Serial Map Service – monthly digest of commentary and maps relating to the Second World War, beginning September 1939. (Phoenix Book Company)

Statistisches Handbuch: Statistical summary covering Germany from 1928 to 1944, produced for the American occupying forces. (Munich, 1949)

Trial of German Major War Criminals: HMSO 1946–50 – verbatim record of the Nuremberg proceedings (22 vols). London.

USSBS: United States Strategic Bombing Survey 1945–7 (208 vols). Washington DC. For a valuable guide to these reports, see Daniels, G. (ed.) (1981). *A Guide to the Reports of the United States Strategic Bombing Survey*. London.

Other published sources

Aleff, E. (no date). *Terror und Widerstand, 1933–45*. Berlin.

Bessel, R. (1984). *Political Violence and the Rise of Nazism: the stormtroopers in eastern Germany, 1925–34*. New Haven.

Billig, J. (1973). *Les camps concentrationaires dans l'économie du Reich Hitlérrien. Paris.*

Broszat, M. (1968). The concentration camps, 1933–45. In Buchheim, H., Broszat, M., Krausnick, H. and Jacobson, H. A. (eds) *Anatomy of the SS State*. London.

Broszat, M. (1981). *The Hitler State: the foundation and development of the internal structure of the Third Reich*. London.

Burchardt, L. (1985). The impact of the war economy on the civilian population of Germany during the First and Second World Wars. In Deist, W. (ed.) *The German Military in the Age of Total War*. Leamington.

Coon, C. S. (1939). *The Races of Europe*. New York.

Dallin, A. (1957). *German Rule in Russia, 1941–5 – a study of occupation policies*. London.

de Martonne, E. (1930). *L'Europe Central*, vol 4. Paris.

Dickinson, R. E. (1938). The economic regions of Germany. *Geographical Review* **28**: 609–26.

Farquharson, J. (1976). *The Plough and the Swastika: the NSDAP and agriculture in Germany, 1928–1945*. London.

Forstmeier, F. and Volkmann, H. E. (1977) (eds). *Kriegswirtschaft und Rüstung, 1939–45*. Düsseldorf.

Gilbert, E. W. (1941). *How the Map has Changed, 1938–1940*. Oxford

Gilbert, M. (1978). *The Holocaust*. London.

Goodall, M. A. (1941) (ed.). *The War in Maps*. London.

Grünberger, R. (1970). *Hitler's SS*. London.

Grunfeld, F. V. (1974). *The Hitler File: a social history of Germany and the Nazis, 1918–45*. London.

Hayes, P. (1987). *Industry and Ideology: I-G Farben in the Nazi Era*. Cambridge.

Hewitt, K. (1983). Place annihilation: area bombing and the fate of the urban places. *Annals of the Association of American Geographers* **73**: 257–84.

Hilberg, R. (1961). *The Destruction of the European Jews*. Chicago.

Hilgemann, W. (1984). *Atlas zur deutschen Zeitgeschichte, 1918–1968*. Munich.

Hinz, B. (1979). *Art in the Third Reich*. Oxford.

Horrabin, J. (1940–6). *An Atlas History of the Second Great War* (10 vols). London.

Kater, M. (1983). *The Nazi Party: a social profile of members and leaders, 1919–1945*. Oxford.

Klein, B. H. (1959). *Germany's economic preparations for war*. Cambridge, Massachusetts.

Koehl, R. L. (1983). *The Black Corps: the structure and power struggles of the Nazi SS*. Madison, Wisconsin.

Kuhnrich, H. (1983). *Die KPD im Kampf gegen die faschistische Diktatur, 1933–45*. Berlin.

Kulischer, E. M. (1943). *The Displacement of Population in Europe*. Montreal.

Kwiet, K. and Eschwege, H. (1984). *Selbstbehauptung und Widerstand: Deutsche Juden im Kampf um Existenz und Menschenwurde*, 1933–45. Hamburg.

Mammoch, K. (1984). *Widerstand, 1933–39*. Berlin.

Milatz, A. (1965). *Wähler und Wahlen in der Weimarer Republik*. Bonn.

Milward, A. S. (1977). *War, Economy and Society, 1939–45*. London.

Noakes, J. and Pridham, G. (1974) (eds). *Documents on Nazism*. London.

Noakes, J. and Pridham, G. (1984) (eds). *Nazism, 1919–45: a documentary reader, vol. 2: State, Economy and Society, 1933–39*. Exeter.

Orlow, D. (1971, 1973). *The History of the Nazi Party, 1919–1945* (2 vols). Newton Abbot.

Petzina, D. (1968). *Autarkiepolitik im Dritten Reich: der national-sozialistische Vierjahresplan*. Stuttgart.

Pfahlmann, H. (1964). *Fremdarbeiter und Kriegsgefangene in der deutschen Kriegswirtschaft, 1939–45*. Würzburg.

Stolper, G. (1940). *German Economy, 1870–1940: issues and trends*. New York.

Volkmann, H. E. (1977). NS-Aussenhandel im 'geschlossen' Kriegswirtschaftraum 1939–41. In Forstmeier and Volkmann, *Kriegswirtschaft – und Rüstung*, pp. 113.

Wagenführ, R. (1963). *Die deutsche Industrie im Kriege 1939–45*. Berlin.

Wittmann, K. (1977). *Deutsch-schwedische Wirtschaftsbeziehungen im Zweiten Weltkrieg*. In Forstmeier and Volkmann, *Kriegswirtschaft und Rüstung*, pp. 203.

Select bibliographical guide

The following list provides suggestions for further reading for those unfamiliar with the history of the Third Reich. It is confined to books; for guidance on the voluminous periodical literature, readers should consult the recent historiographic surveys.

The Weimar Republic

Eyck, E. (1962, 1964). *A History of the Weimar Republic* (2 vols). Oxford.

Hiden, J. (1974). *The Weimar Republic*. London.

Nicholls, A. J. (1991). *Weimar and the Rise of Hitler*, 3rd edn. London.

Peukert, D. J. K. (1991). *The Weimar Republic*. London.

General and introductory accounts on Hitler and the Third Reich

Bullock, A. (1962). *Hitler: a study in tyranny*. London.

Kershaw, I. (1987). *The 'Hitler Myth': image and reality in the Third Reich*. London.

Shirer, W. L. (1960). The Rise and Fall of the Third Reich. London

Trevor-Roper, H. R. (1987). *The Last Days of Hitler*, 6th edn. London.

Williamson, D. G. (1982). *The Third Reich*. London.

Recent surveys and reviews of the historical literature

Frei, N. (1993). *National Socialist Rule in Germany: the Fuehrer state, 1933–45*. Oxford.

Hiden, J. and Farquharson, J. (1989). *Explaining Hitler's Germany*, 2nd edn. London.

Hildebrand, K. (1984) *The Third Reich*. London.

Kershaw, I. (1993). *The Nazi Dictatorship: problems and perspectives of interpretation*, 3rd edn. London.

Laqueur, W. (1979) (ed.). *Fascism: a reader's guide*. London.

Some major perspectives on the Third Reich

Bracher, K. D. (1971). *The German Dictatorship: the origins, structure and consequences of National Socialism.* London.

Broszat, M. (1981). *The Hitler State: the foundation and development of the internal structure of the Third Reich.* London.

Burleigh, M. and Wippermann, W. (1991). *The Racial State: Germany, 1933–1945.* Cambridge.

Hirschfeld, G. and Kettenacker, L. (1981) (eds). *Der 'Führerstaat': Mythos und Realitat.* Stuttgart.

Neumann, F. (1942). *Behemoth: the structure and practice of National Socialism.* London.

Rich, N. (1973, 1974). *Hitler's War Aims* (2 vols). London.

The Nazi Party

Hamilton, R. F. (1982). *Who Voted for Hitler.* Princeton.

Kater, M. (1983). *The Nazi Party: a social profile of members and leaders, 1919–45.* Oxford.

Orlow, D. (1971, 1973). *The History of the Nazi Party, 1919–1945* (2 vols). Newton Abbot.

Society under Nazism

Bessel, R. (1987) (ed.). *Life in the Third Reich.* Oxford.

Grünberger, R. (1971). *A Social History of the Third Reich.* London.

Hinz, B. (1979). *Art in the Third Reich.* Oxford.

Mosse, G. L. (1966). *Nazi Culture.* London.

Peukert, D. J. K. (1987). *Inside Nazi Germany: conformity, opposition and racism in everyday life.* Oxford.

Schoenbaum, D. (1967). *Hitler's Social Revolution: class and status in Nazi Germany, 1933–9.* London.

Stachura, P. D. (1978) (ed.). *The Shaping of the Nazi State.* London.

Economy under Nazism (including the war)

Forstmeier, F. and Volkmann, H. E. (1977) (eds). *Kriegswirtschaft und Rüstung, 1939–45.* Düsseldorf.

Gillingham, J. R. (1985). *Industry and Politics in the Third Reich: Ruhr coal, Hitler and Europe.* London.

Hayes, P. (1987). *Industry and Ideology: I G Farben in the Nazi era.* Cambridge.

Milward, A. S. (1965). *The German Economy at War.* London.

Milward, A. S. (1977). *War, Economy and Society, 1939–45*. London.

Nathan, O. (1944). *The Nazi Economic System: Germany's mobilisation for war*. Durham, North Carolina.

Overy, R. J. (1982). *The Nazi Economic Recovery, 1932–8*. London.

Overy, R. J. (1994). *War and Economy in the Third Reich*. Oxford.

Petzina, D. (1968). *Autarkiepolitik im Dritten Reich: der national-sozialistische Vierjahresplan*. Stuttgart.

Wagenführ, R. (1963). *Die deutsche Industrie im Kriege 1939–45*. Berlin.

The army

Cooper, M. (1978). *The German Army, 1933–45: its political and military failure*. London.

Deist, W. (1985) (ed.). *The German Military in the Age of Total War*. Leamington.

O'Neill, R. J. (1966). *The German Army and the Nazi Party, 1933–9*. London.

The SS and the war machine

Breitman, R. (1991). *The Architect of Genocide: Himmler and the final solution*. Oxford.

Buchheim, H., Broszat, M., Krausnick, H. and Jacobsen, H. A. (1968). *Anatomy of the SS State*. London.

Dallin, A. (1957). *German Rule in Russia, 1941–5: a study of occupation policies*. London.

Gellately, R. (1990). *The Gestapo and German Society: enforcing racial policy, 1933–1945*. Oxford.

Georg, E. (1962). *Die wirtschaftlichen Unternehmungen der SS*. Stuttgart.

Gilbert, M. (1978) *The Holocaust*. London.

Hilberg, R. (1961). *The Destruction of the European Jews*. Chicago.

Homze, E. L. (1967). *Foreign Labour in Nazi Germany*. Princeton.

Koehl, R. L. (1983). *The Black Corps: the structure and power struggles of the Nazi SS*. Madison, Wisconsin.

Kogon, E. (1950). *The Theory and Practice of Hell*. London.

Laqueur, W. (1980). *The Terrible Secret*. London.

Reitlinger, G. (1956). *The SS: alibi of a nation, 1922–45*. London.

Speer, A. (1981). *The Slave State: Heinrich Himmler's master plan for SS supremacy*. London.

Geographical accounts of Germany in the Nazi era

The British *Admiralty Handbooks* (see under references) summarise a vast body of English and German contemporary material. Other useful works are:

Dickinson, R. E. (1963). *Germany*. London.

Mellor, R. E. H. (1978). *The Two Germanies* (part I). London.
An atlas of modern German history (in German) which includes much material on the Nazi period is:

Hilgemann, W. (1984). *Atlas zur deutschen Zeitgeschichte, 1918–1968*. Munich.

Reference works on Nazi Germany

Kirk, T. (1994). *The Longman Companion to Nazi Germany*. London.

Noakes, J. and Pridham, G. (1983–8) (eds). *Nazism, 1919–45: a documentary reader* (3 vols). Exeter.

Glossary

Altreich Old Reich – term used by Nazis to refer to the land area of Germany before 1938

Einsatzgruppen Commando groups – special Gestapo and SS 'killing' squads

Freikorps Free Corps – volunteer defence units organised by former army officers from 1918

Gaue Regions – the name given to the regional/territorial divisions of the Nazi Party

Gauleiter Region leader – the Nazi Party's regional/territorial leader

Gleichschaltung Political co-ordination – the process whereby all institutions and organisations were harnessed in the service of Nazism

Herrenvolk Master race or master people – part of Nazi racial terminology

Kampfbund Combat League – association of militant right-wing groups

Kreise Districts – term used to denote area subdivisions of the Party Gaue; used also in local government administration

Kreisleiter District leader – Nazi Party leader in a Kreis

Länder States of the federation – the name given to the former sovereign states of Germany under the Weimar Republic

Reichsbahn German State Railways

Reichsrat State Council – the council or assembly of the Länder under the Weimar Republic

Reichstag Imperial Diet – the German National Assembly or Parliament

Reichswehr Imperial forces – the term used for the German Army until the mid-1930s

Stahlhelm Steel Helmet – Nationalist, ex-soldiers' organisation, founded 1918

Waffen-SS Army formation of SS

Wehrkreise Military districts – the Army's regional administrative divisions

Wehrmacht The German armed forces

Weltanschauung World outlook – the term used in Nazi ideology

Zentrum Catholic Centre Party

Index